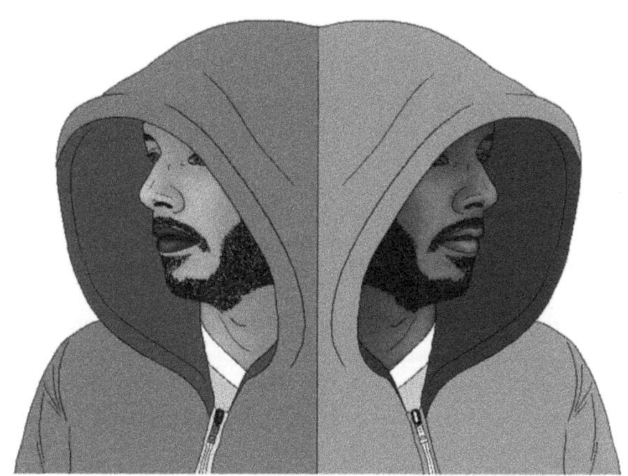

THE REMAINS
OF A HUMAN

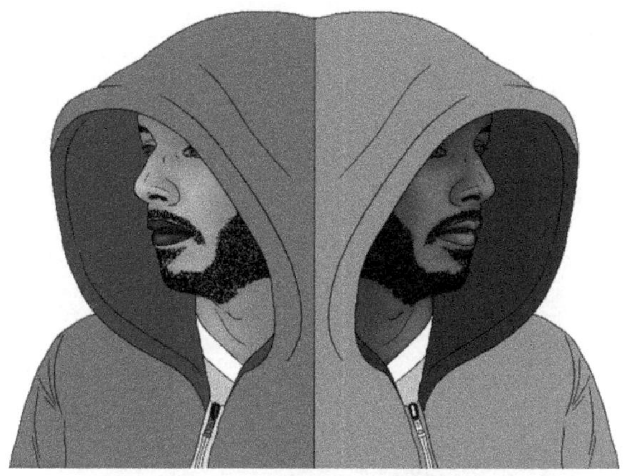

THE REMAINS OF A HUMAN

Poetry by
ADRIC CENERI

A tribute to a decade since his birth as a poet.

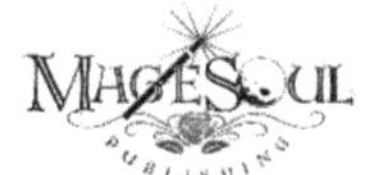

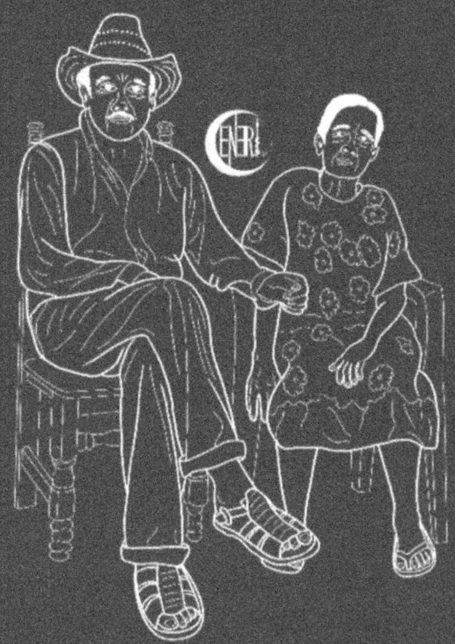

I want to dedicate this book to my grandparents.

My grandpa visited me last night in my dreams, I was talking to him about my first book, 'my poetry', and how excited I have been feeling for this year, marking a decade of my birth as a published poet and author. I was telling him of my hesitated idea about rewriting and re-editing my first book for a second publication but separating the Spanish version from the English version. My grandpa with a big smile and palming my back said, "Go for it, SPLIT the book" and I woke up.

I present to you the English version:

The Remains of a Human

*To my old lady for always giving herself
fully and completely to her grandkids.
I will never forget you,
I will never forget how much you loved me
and how much you cared for my well-being.*

*Wherever you may be,
I know you are watching over me
and I know in my heart that you are so proud of me,
and even if at times I feel broken
for not being able to have done more for you,
I know you understand my reasons, my pains
and your unconditional love
will always remain in my heart.*

*To my old man,
grandpa I know that you loved me in your own way,
you were so loving
and happiness is all I ever remember from you.
Thank you for the guidance
you have given me through my dreams at night.
Thank you for pushing me
and for giving me the hints to clear my doubts
and motivating me to get far.*

*I love you,
always and forever*

your grandson.

Acknowledgements

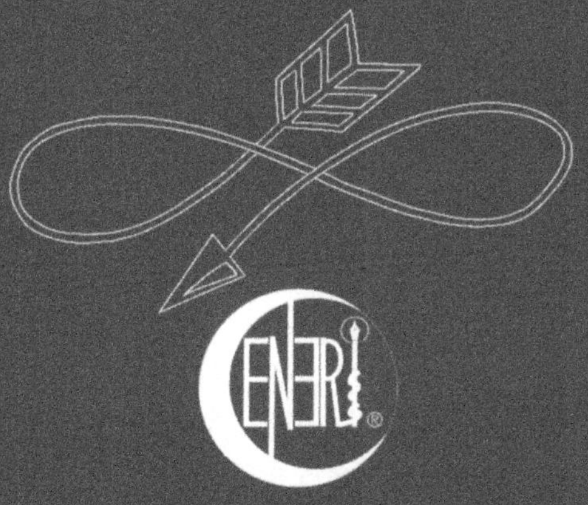

I want to thank my husband for always standing by my side. For giving me the courage and support to continue growing as an artist, as a creator. I can never thank him enough for the unconditional love he provides to my heart.

I also want to thank Nina Mackey for helping me edit this second edition making it a better version than its first publication. I want to thank Carlos Medina for helping me edit and proofread the final manuscript.

And lastly, I want to express my immense gratitude to the publisher, Magesoul Publishing. Thank you for believing in me and my creativity, for giving me a spot in their platform to share my art and poetry with everyone in the poetry community and the whole world.

CONTENTS

MELANCHOLY

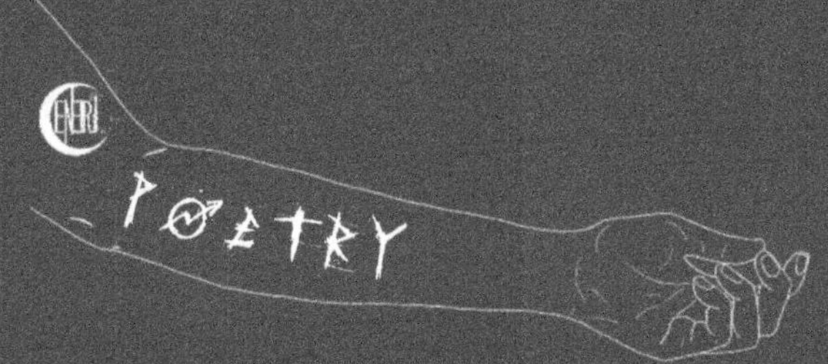

REMAINS

I used to feel, but now I don't!
I used to cry, but now I won't!
I used to be myself, but now I'm not!
I used to see, but now I'm blind!
I used to need, but now I don't!
I used to laugh, but now I won't!
I used to read, but I sold my eyes!
I used to analyze, but I lost my mind!

All this is related. All this is black. Bad advice and thoughts.
I have no need of this in my life.

I want to get rid of this,
no matter who, no matter what.
I just don't want to be who I am now.
The remains of myself are nothing, but pain and sadness.

Life, it's confusing and it confuses my madness.
It confuses my soul and my emptiness.
There's not much left to say,
but to say I'm not myself. I'm lost in my world.

I want to say; the war did not defeat me!
But I want no more lies.
No more crying. No more sorrows. I want to laugh.
I want happiness; I want to feel alive.
I want to travel, to fly around.

Go to Italy; Spain or France,
maybe Argentina or México.
México, I miss you; how can I not?
I miss your beaches, ports and rivers.
I miss that kid; I miss myself,
I have to go and this is the end.

THE REMAINS OF A HUMAN

Every time I wake up…
You're always on my unstable mind!
What have you done to me?

These memories of my childhood
don't let me breathe at all.
They don't let me live without fear,
they don't let me sleep in peace.

The balance of my life
is a total chaos,
is for what people expect of me,
the main reason not to stay here.

Time has flown away,
the truth is, it could never be the same,
all I can do now is escape.

Your tears aren't worthy,
not for my cure, I'll prove you were wrong.
My wounds don't heal,
I'll be back when your eyes get to see I'm real.

What I offer to you is not enough.
I don't want to be an obstacle in your path,
I am just a problem behind this mask.
It's better not to let you know,
that your eyes won't see my face anymore.

I propose myself to walk away from this life,
to erase my pain, to believe in faith.
I will run to the divine line,
to sleep for a while, to wait for an end.

I don't blame anyone for judging me,
because all it is, is ignorance.
I don't blame anyone for killing my soul,
nor for leaving my remains in this world.

I was no more than a lost reason,
one of the many agonies of the forgotten,
one of many dreams unrealized.

Now I leave…
everything stays in its place.
I wish to confront my present,
but I have no strength to fight against it.
I just wish to hide away from everything.

With the sunrise, a new day will come,
with it my life will be history,
lines of a verse, the feelings of my story.

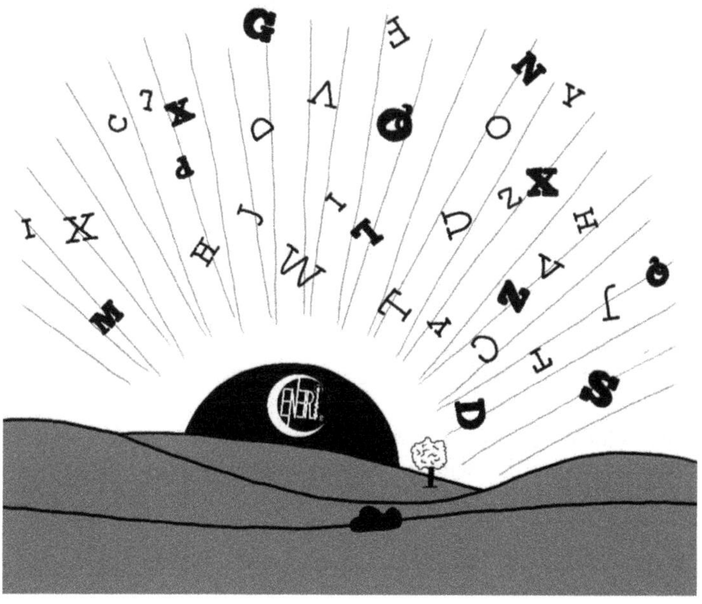

I USED TO

I used to believe that life was always the present.
Now I know that a tomorrow will be here,
although I'll be absent.
In the tomorrow, few people will be there.
By then, the rest will be just memories in minds.
Life keeps on its way and never stops.
Sometimes I am more afraid to live
than to be in hell with Death.
As for people like me,
life is always more difficult and different.

I used to think that life was always filled with happiness.
Then I realized life
has many issues, such as pain and sorrow.
Life is based on good and evil.
So, I always take it as a game,
where no one knows who's going to get the prize.

I used to wish to be old enough.
So I could enjoy freedom and life.
Now I know, I should've never thought of that.
As every moment is at its time
and every piece is in its place.
It's like wanting to run, before knowing how to walk.
These are nature's things and steps of life we can't skip,
because every single step has a goal to reach.

I used to be afraid of people
and wondered, "What will they say?"

Now, in these times I really don't care.
I have learned to live with what I have
and the feelings I don't trust.

As many times, feelings trick us and hurt our hearts.
At the end, the wounds are difficult to heal,
that is why I'm aware to be careful
and not to let myself get too into it.

My world used to be black and white,
making my life's fake.

I told myself to leave that place.
At the age I was supposed to be playing,
I did things at the wrong moment.
I made mistakes, which were giving me a hard time.
When I got rid of them,
it was too late to notice
that my innocence was falling apart.

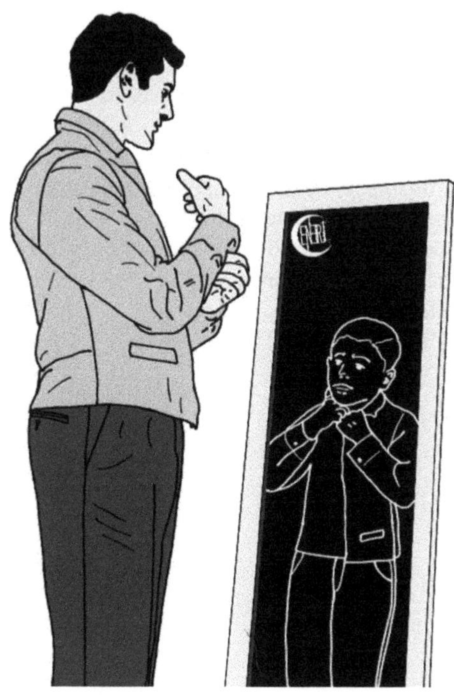

HATE UNDER THE PEACE

The moments are already gone,
but the memories won't leave.
The lost souls from the Forgotten don't seem to come back.

I once had a father. Before no one knew, he just forgot.
He forgot he had a son. He pretended it never happened.

I once traveled and I got lost.
I walked parts of the world.
I walked around many seas. I roamed in the streets.

I once asked for a wish. A wish that turned into a nightmare.
I wanted to have parents. I wanted the love of a family.

I once thought not to be. But escaping was never the answer.
And even if wars seize peace,
there's no reason to wish not to exist.

Now, I just only think one thing.
End this misery, which makes me feel incomplete.
This crazy idea, the idea to be,
to have my childhood back and once again be a kid.
The happy kid as I never was.
Time took my dream,
now I'm alone as I've always been.

PERHAPS

Perhaps I don't belong in here,
who could know the truth of this?
Maybe the Sky who claims its winds,
who knows of this eclipse?

Emptiness is what I deeply feel,
these awful nightmares and scary screams!
I feel to give up hope,
than to keep on waiting for the Lord!

Nor you or I will ever be able to change my past.
I think at least I deserve some peace.
I don't blame anyone for what I was,
but myself and these uninvited lies.

Hell not know and shall you'll never see,
it's confuse and it will all end here.
My misery is trapped and I wouldn't let free,
I might no longer exist but it all will be as it should.

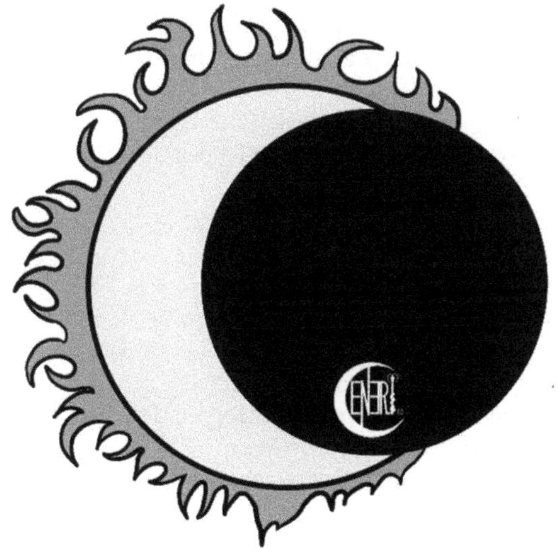

LOST

As I begin to think about so many things,
so many times, so much time, it's hard for me to forget.

How is it possible to pretend that you never existed?
I cannot fake this as if I didn't adore you,
as if I didn't want you.

I still yearn for you because I loved you,
I love you and I will always love you!

Your caresses are unforgettable, your hugs.
It was your presence that made every moment special,
life always goes on, but without you nothing is the same.

Each smile... that with an internal brightness gave life
even to the most boring moments.
You... who never turned back, you flew,
traveled and you always went where you wanted to go.

Why don't you do it now?
What happened with your indomitable wings
and the unfriendly cynicism of society?

What happened to the rebellious child?
What happened to the infinite desire to succeed?

You are not that rugrat anymore...
The fantasies stayed in the past,
you no longer believe in ideas,
Life has abused you beyond count.

Lost in an empty reality you stayed,
it's sad to see that you've accepted defeat,
that your desire to live is over,
on a notebook in a lost page.

CHAPTER 2

ACHING SORROWS

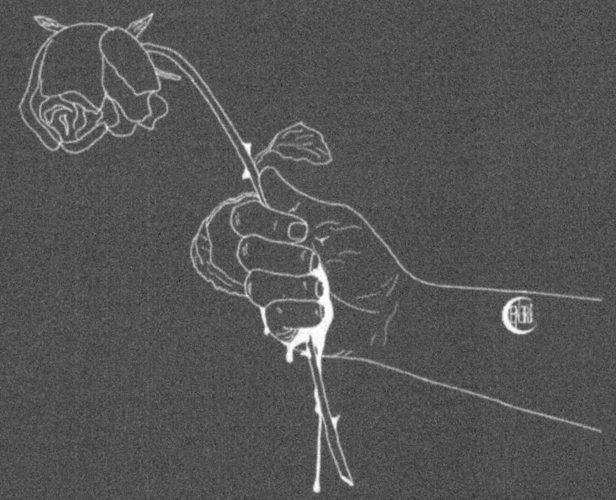

MORTALITY

It seems that time takes advantages over life,
although, I'm at peace with my soul.
Looks like I'm losing the battle,
but the war is not yet won.

The end is getting closer,
day after day I am weaker.
I'm so close to the eternal dream,
far away from the wished peace.

Obstacles in my path don't have an end,
the sky is sad and cries for my remains.
Far away is distance, far away there is no trust.

I walked over the fire. I slept in the mountains.
Mountains of problems, problems with no end.

The squall hits my back as I pay for my punishment.
The water swallows me, it takes everything I ever had.

I believe there's no escape,
to not die… impossible to run from destiny,
impossible when you have a mortality.

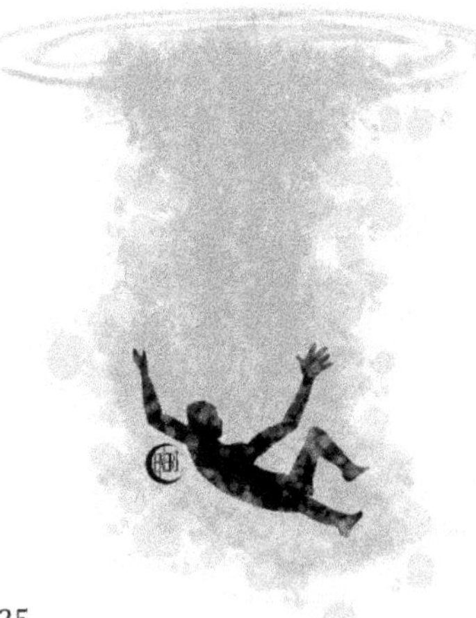

FATAL ACCIDENT

The Fall has come,
with deep coldness and so much pain.
The leaves of the trees fall down
with the cold Winter winds.

I can remember it,
as if it happened only yesterday.
What difficult times!
So confused with all these things in my life.
Being on a path,
where you can't choose to leave or to stay
is like being in a place
where your thoughts have no say.
For some reason,
all this happened and we couldn't prevent it.

It's almost six o'clock…
Lightning falls down with great shiver and noise.
The rain falls down and there's only just pain.
The broken crystals and irons are crossing my body.
My sight is suddenly fading away.
The pain is too strong.
I fight to stay.
The pain is stronger than me.

I open my eyes and all I see is light.
Light everywhere, I'm lost in light.

"Am I dead?"
— "I don't think so! I can't be."
The confusion makes me crazy.
I want to cry
because I'm really afraid.

There are no more tears in my eyes.
I stay in silence.
I don't know what to do!
I want to believe I'm alive.
The doubts have taken my faith away.
I fall down, I can't stay awake.

Finally, I wake up again.
What a deep and cruel pain.
I want to say this once
before the pain takes me away again.

I want to have the opportunity
to see him one more time.
Hopefully, he listens to me!
It's almost the end.
I'm weak and I can't stay awake,
I'm afraid this is my end!

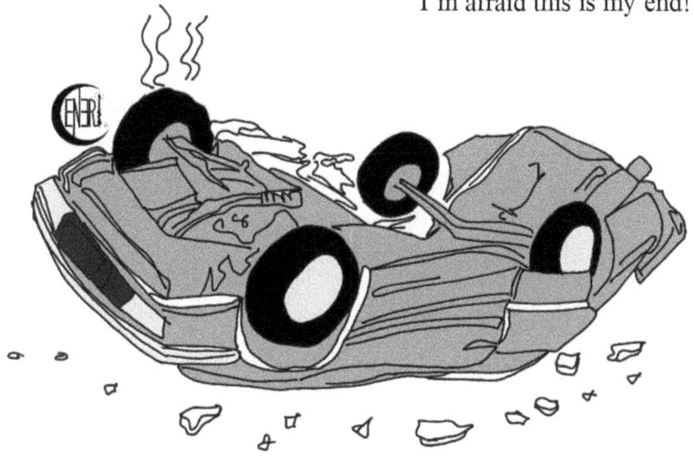

LOST THOUGHTS

Time always fades away,
I still remember it as if it happened yesterday.
I believe now it doesn't matter…
Not now, not ever – it's too late.

And what hurts the most is to know
who did it, why did they did it.
And because of it, I am a lost boy.

What I've lost is lost,
now it can only be true in my thoughts.
The wind has blown my broken heart away,
to avoid seeing its pain every day.
As I think of my childhood, I feel nostalgic…
I wish to be, to have me back, to be innocent.

For sure, I now understand,
you can't just find love anywhere,
it has to be earned and nurtured with care.

What I've been fed
has turned me into a damaged being.
I've lost everything
and ended up walking deserts alone.
I tasted life's sourest flavor
while my family was gone.

I have created a world full of lies,
but at the end, everything falls down,
faith has no doubts…
Faith beseeched upon pain and love,
feelings of a scared soul,
someone different… a unique boy.

It's better to live peacefully
and ignore my suffering,
time always walks away and life is never fair.

Make of yourself the best and worst,
forget about everything – enjoy the world,
because that's what God made it for.

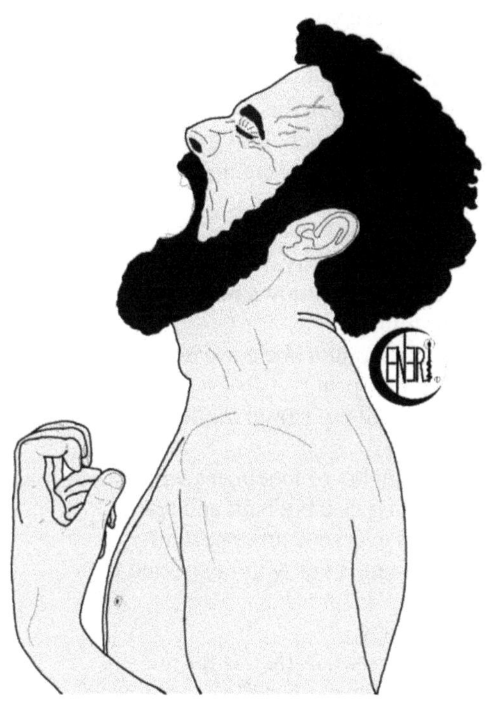

IT'S NOT THAT EASY

There are no longer nights
than the ones you're not here.
There is no colder sadness
than letting you leave.

I want to erase your memories from mind.
I want to learn how to say goodbye
without showing my tears.
There is nobody in this world,
nobody who can get close to me.
There is no space for me in this world,
I can't do anything.

If I could control my destiny,
no one would've known me.
In your mind,
I probably wouldn't be a memory.
I would disappear
along with all my stupid motives.

The long nights of loneliness without you, right here,
with nothing else but pain and tears.
Life gives everyone an opportunity,
but who I am is not who I expected to be!

I'm not happy.
I don't know what life has for me.
I wonder if, in another life,
I was a bad guy.

As far as I remember, I have never been an angel,
nor an evil demon who destroys everything.
I understand that life is a beautiful gift,
no one should waste their given time.

Life gives and takes away;
it makes us poor but sometimes rich.
Life is hard to understand
that now and then I wish to kill myself.

I can be a rebel, funny, extreme, and more than that,
but at times even heroes need of someone.
No one survives the ugly reality.

Death comes and takes us, families cry,
but memories fade over time.
I don't know what to do, what to say,
or if I want to be awake.
Life is so strange, so cruel,
so cold, and full of grace.

I have never thought of doing what I do, nor to go as far as I
have come. I hear sounds that flood my mind of memories,
words, which stayed in my soul, illusions, which I wonder if
they could be more than just words.

Dreams and nightmares inside my unstable mind,
it is true, life isn't what we always want.
Neither rich nor poor people
— no one escapes from the devil.
Life is so strange, so beautiful, so sweet,
and so evil.

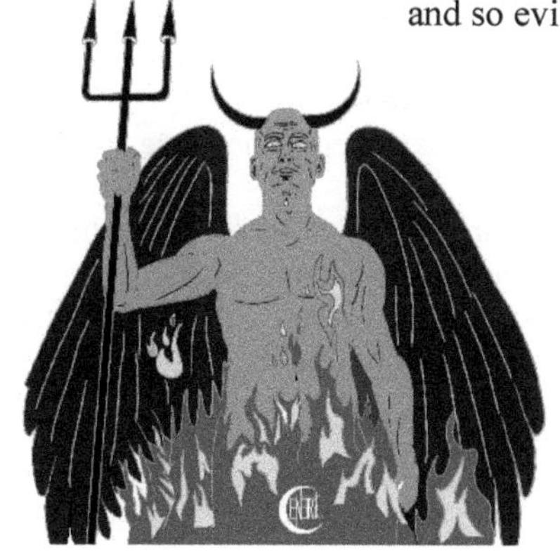

A LOST SOLDIER

You grew up alone, confused and lost.
Paris streets were your beautiful home.
You believe God took away everything from you,
your illusions of a lover who didn't return.

There's nothing left… only ashes,
the dust of memories fueled by painful sorrows.
Sitting in a chair, looking away, you cry…
Tears of moments saved in your mind,
lived long ago in the city of Berlin, Germany.

Ancient Greece… city where you loved him,
when you barely were a boy.
His caresses of love
are just memories buried in your essence.

A surprise to know that, although he was a soldier,
it didn't stop him from approaching you
to reveal his darkest secrets,
details of problems never mentioned to anyone before.

He loved you beyond the sunset and sunrise,
beyond the truth and lies…

Oh, poor child…
It's sad to see how time fades away.
Still sadder to see
how life takes your innocence away.

The wind comes to you and laughs
continuously over and over,
saying all you wished for that one day
but today is not that day.

You never thought this dream would be over,
but illusions come and go, as do lovers.
You might move far away from this continent,
but you will always have him in your memories.

You are going to start a new life,
but be sure that he'll always be in your heart.
Maybe you'll never mention him again,
but forever you'll remember his touch on your skin.

In his tomb, the soldier laid,
now that you've started your new life.
It's a shame that he couldn't have stayed,
time is never fair and it's too late to cry.

Maybe it was him,
the person who manifested your childhood,
he represented something beautiful to you.
You might love someone else one day,
but not the special way you loved him.

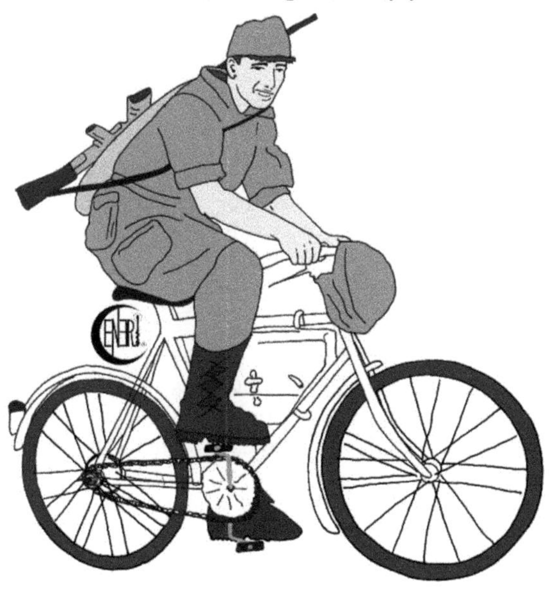

RESIGNATION TO LOSE YOU

Somehow at some point I came to terms with losing you,
to lose those memories,
those caresses, hugs and kisses.

Between today and always,
reality is a different thing.

How could I make it?
What do I get for loving you?
If we both know you rejected me!

I am not the problem… No!
My heart is the problem.
This piece of meat that beats fast as light-peed,
it makes my life stay lost in dreams.

I wish to leave you but I just can't…
I do love you.
Don't walk away…
My feelings don't seem to fade.

My love for you is so much stronger
than the same loneliness,
much higher than Everest,
and as big as the Sahara Desert.
This willing to see you one more time,
tolerate more of your obstinate mind.
I believe you, but my heart doesn't,
I write it here… I can't face you.

This is my farewell to our friendship,
I don't think of my love to you as a mistake,
but I now know that you weren't my soulmate.

I guess you could have loved me,
but not the way I expected.
Now I have to fix my broken heart.
The ink of my pen is finished,
and my heart doesn't seem to heal.

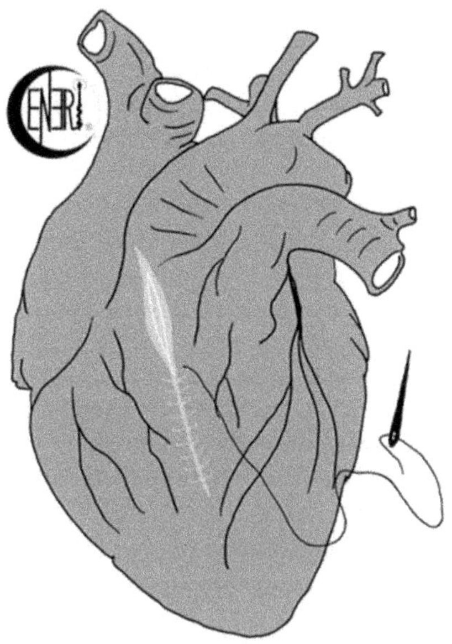

ALONE WITHOUT YOU

I lived amongst lies. In the mirror's reflection,
I spent days and nights.
Locked in a closet where I had no life.

I got tired of this sacrifice,
tired of moving at your pace.
I love you as much as alcoholics love wine,
but my reasoning is far logical than my blind heart.

I don't feel satisfied with you at all,
I don't see a future between you and me.
You're the traitor… you lost my trust,
I gave you love and you despised me.

The things you offered me,
anyone can give, without thinking twice.
Be sure that I will always remember you.
But remember that you will never be back in my arms.

The sensual movement of your hands
doesn't provoke me anymore.

I offered you my whole life;
I realized that no one values it enough.
I realized that I am better without your lies.

I now understand your underlined fear.
It's a shame that it must ends like this,
when yesterday we were perfect for each other,
but today, I can't force myself to be your lover.
I am out of words for this conversation,
and for sure, I know it's not you I'm in love with.

Finally, today I have my life back.
I return to my house,
with my wife… my beautiful Soledad.

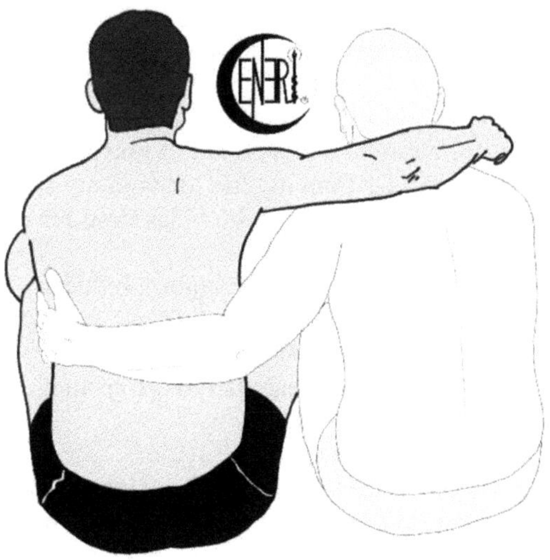

ALL I WANT

Today, all I want is to fly.
I want to know what it feels to fall apart,
to know what is like to fade away,
feel afraid of my future as I run away.

I want to feel lost between loneliness,
I don't want to be with you in this horrible hell,
I want to run far from my life to avoid my suffering,
I want to be the coward, who hides from his reality.

I want to sell my soul to the highest bidder,
I feel worthless as you slowly kill me with your love.
The starry night saddens…
as it sees my painful tears fall to the ground.

I wish to believe in you once again,
but you preferred to throw my love into the ocean,
knowing my soul didn't know how to swim.

I'm in pain, and you can't imagine
how much this emptiness hurts,
it hurts more now that you've gone away,
now that I know that I will never see you again.

Once again, the night is starry,
it cries with me as we see my memories vanish,
as I figured out you never loved me…
I hurt myself, as I remember that for you,
my life I would have given away.

As I know you lied to me
and that I always gave you reasons to trust me.
As I feel you hurt me,
and the wounds don't want to heal.

As I think I loved you,
I realized that your love was never real.
As I know you left me,
I know you won't come back.

As I hear the night, she says you don't deserve me,
another person will mend my heart.
You're inhumane,
you never felt, you have no heart.

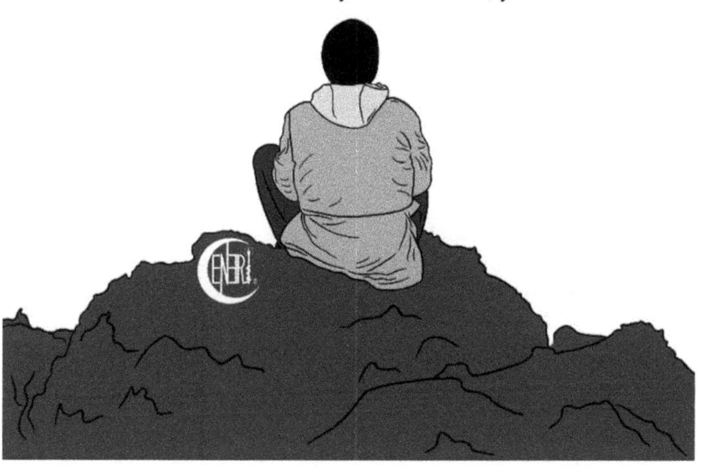

CONFUSION

I'm so confused
and I don't know which way to go.
I believed I knew the answers, but I don't know.

I believed I knew who I was,
but now I don't know who I am.
I'm lost in a perception,
in here, the questions pound in my mind.

I'm lost in a maze,
lost between the edges of my stress.
I don't know where to go,
nor if I want to stay in this hell.

There's no way to go back
to the place everything started. I'm on a loose string,
I'm at the edge of my abyss.

I can't be myself.
I can't because I don't know who I am.
I used to believe I was invincible,
slowly, but surely, I destroyed myself.
I ripped my heart and my soul faded away.

I'm just tired of acting; I hate to fake feelings.
I'm just a teen boy,
a human being who demands peace and love.

I CAN'T HOLD YOU BACK

Once I was a little kid, who came out of his world for you.
Now, I decided to leave you because you were never true.
"Prince Charming" is just a dream,
a lost wish that's gone.
I feel I have nothing to give, I don't believe anymore.
The starry night laughs at me.
It's cruel but I know that's sadly true.

I give up. I can't fight with a broken heart.
I don't want anything but you, sweetheart.
I had to leave because
we both know
this situation – it's too hard.
It's hard to do this, when we don't know what we want.
We might like each other, but this is not what I want.
I want you to love me, and I can't keep holding you back.

I understand one thing, if you're mine, you'll come back.
If not, there is nothing.
Please don't turn around.
I can't let you watch me cry.
So just leave me… don't ever come back.

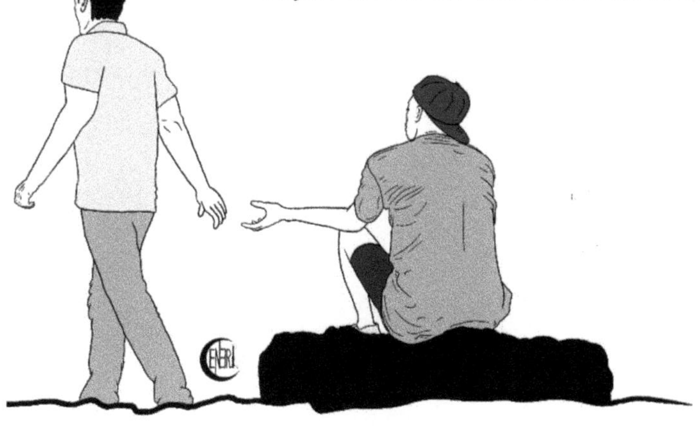

IT HURTS TO REMEMBER

It hurts to remember...
I can almost hear your beautiful words that the sea drowned,
along with you and your desire to love.

Today, as I remember you, I start crying,
because I know that you are not with me anymore.

I know that even if I try to forget you,
I will never achieve it.

You will always be the love of my life...
without thinking, here my love, I wait for you.

If you don't come back, I will seek you,
because I need my soul,
that you took with you when you left
and to this day you still haven't come back.

Just the thought of you never returning to my arms,
many times, I have tried to commit suicide.

I just wanted to see if I could reach you that way,
for the two of us finally could live a peaceful life,
either here on earth or in the next life,
from today... until eternity.

LONGING

Sometimes I dream of myself during my childhood... happy,
I am very happy to have someone to smile with.
I'm with my mom, my little sister and my dad,
we love each other, we play and we enjoy our lives,
happy moments that for some reason,
we will always carry in our hearts.

At the end and without realizing it,
I wake up and I know I have to face my fears,
and I scream until my conscience wins.

Something that took away my sadness came to an end, and now I
return to this world that terrifies me. It was only a dream, that for
a few minutes filled me with consolation.

Now I sit down and analyze my dream,
thinking and remembering the beautiful moments,
that I managed to lived,
moments that vanished with the wind...
now they're only memories.

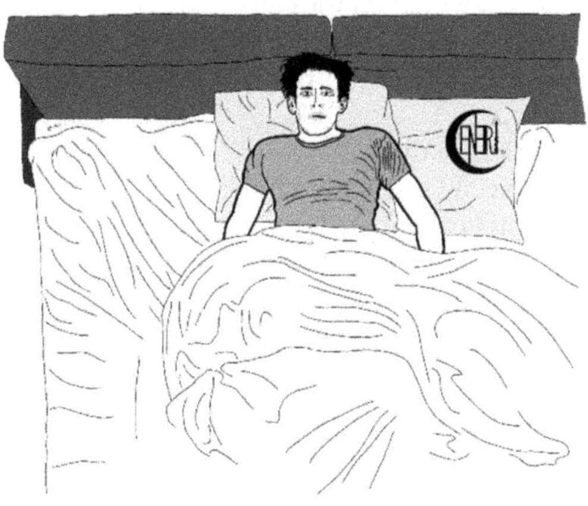

AUDACITY

The stars have six peaks,
glass corners that cut like swords.

The moon is very romantic,
but in the end, we are always hurt by her threats,
we are hurt by the promises sworn before her,
those words that destroyed our soul.

Your caresses tear me apart,
they steal my passion,
my breaths and hopes.

Not thinking about my pain just proves
I love you more than my own life,
your silence, and your ruts hurt me,
they make me dream in a bed of thorns.

Maybe you don't care,
but for you I would give my life.
I've shown you millions of times,
how far I would go for you,
I have shown you in a thousand ways
how much I love you're worthy to me.

Sometimes I think...
that maybe I'm a fool to think,
that you love me in your own way,
that I don't see beyond my wishful dream.
And in spite of everything,
I love you in this special way.

SECLUDED

I thought I knew what I wanted for me,
but now I know that I lost that thought.

I don't think I can feel more pain than the pain I'm feeling,
I am farther from heaven and closer to hell.

The only thing I always dreamed of was being happy.
Was that too much to ask? I don't think so…
However, my hopes have already been lost.

I thought I was capable of loving
until my last breath,
but this confusion is stronger than me,
it's very tense delirium.

It's like feeling the pain when you slit your wrists,
to see the bloodshed alone in the darkness.

I could almost die in agony from this regret,
but who truly cares whether I am asleep or awake?
It doesn't matter if I die,
if in spite of everything I don't return,
and of this trip there remains only a vile and cold body.

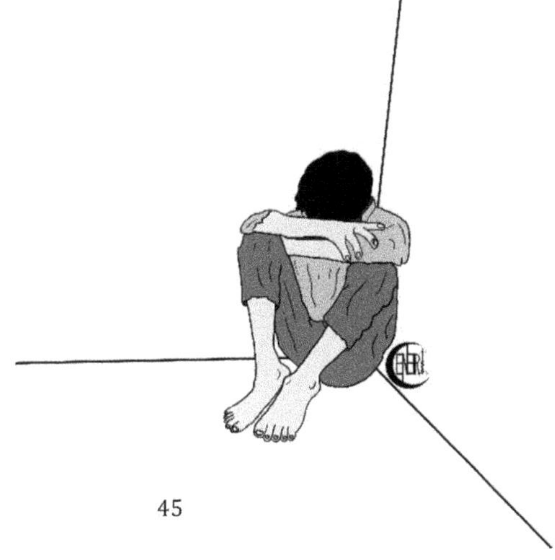

AWAKENING

It's sad to wake up
from a dream that seems so beautiful and real,
to return to the true world,
which for me is hell.

In which I have lived
fighting in oblivion,
Alone... how they left me
and in the oblivion, they buried me.

The people I loved most
wounded me,
now I live with the pain,
searching for a better destiny.

Something that can get me out of this hell...
that tortures me,
I'm sinking
into a swamp of despair,
although the only way out
is death in this life.

Because I cannot longer stand...
neither the pain nor the fatigue.

My heart can no longer resist
another wound in this life.

FORGIVE ME

I may not be the best of all poets,
but from the depths of my soul I give you two roses;
one for when you are feeling sad
and the other to tell you how beautiful you are.

I ask God to bless you,
asking him to always illuminate your path.
I know you're not my only friend,
but in my life, you are someone special.

Friend, I don't know how to explain to you,
how can I tell you that I'm truly sorry for hurting you!
For wanting to help you with your love life,
I almost lost the friendship we have.

Accept my apologies and let's leave this behind,
I promise not to disappoint you,
I will not do it one more time.
I hope our friendship grows
and that you and I remain the same
for the next decades to come.

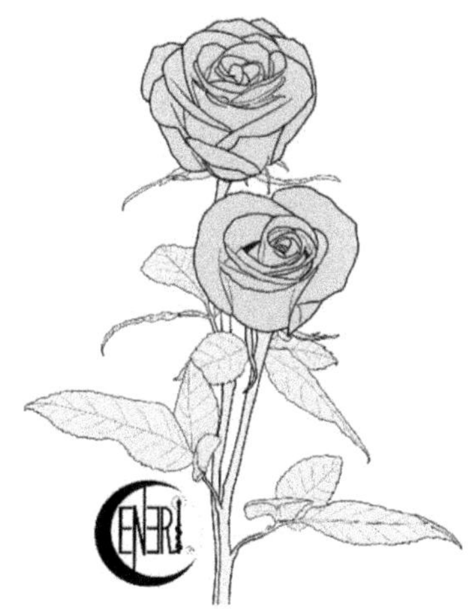

CONCLUSIONS

These are very small roads that will soon end,
profound lovers of the sky, love stories without ends.

Bonds of love, caresses and kisses,
full moons and total eclipses.
Old dreams with never-ending joy,
different cultures and desire to love,
eternal promises
without knowing if they will be fulfilled.

Doubts towards life and who to love,
The raindrops of confusion will fall...
the memories of other places, times without malice.

The caresses and kisses of whom I shouldn't touch,
eternal sins that a piano play when sobbing,
deciphering in each key, each word,
a melody of what they will say,
overcoming tragedies of the past.

I have two pains, bad memories and heartbreak,
the silver moon binds me to his path,
to follow her forever with vain illusions,
it's true, life and every beginning have an end,
My end is not near, it's not my turn to fly yet.

CHAPTER 3

DISDAINS

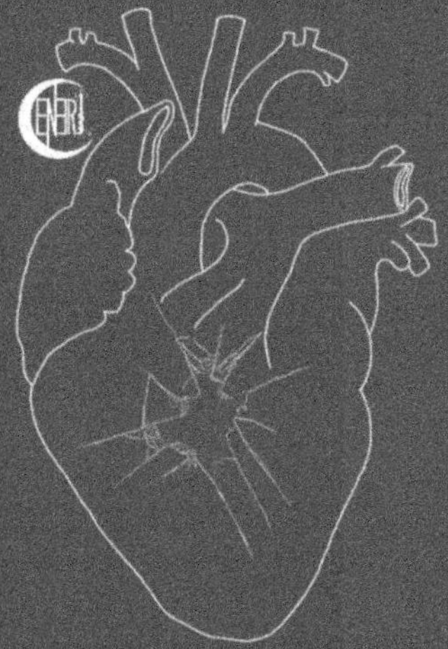

GREAT EXPECTATIONS

I wish I knew how not to think of you,
but it's not possible – you're always on my mind.

Seems you're like the breath that gives me life,
and with your contempt, you break my heart.

I wish I could change my name and life,
be someone else, a better human.
I want to forget you,
the world, and even my mother
but I am not sure if I can do it.

I'm not sure about getting rid of everything
and starting all over.

I've seen myself fail so many times,
falling once again won't make me die.
This is normal and the routine of my heart.

Once I thought love was one of the best feelings ever.
I was wrong and sincerely falling in love is not clever.

I don't know what to do;
I'm waiting for answers,
clues to all my concerns.

It's not my fault
that I am who I am today it doesn't matter,
I hate people who smile at me – they're hypocrites.

When I see hypocrites, I just contain myself,
I smile, watch and walk away.

I want to scream but I'm afraid,
I just want to fly, to travel far away.
Be as simple and light as the wind,
be like the clouds of the sky that venture to the west.

Slowly and softly disappear
until there's nothing left of myself.

I just want to be who I've always dreamt of being,
I just want to be happy but like this I won't ever be.

I'm sorry; it's too cruel, and too real.
If I learned something from life,
it was to be who I am today but as far as I see,
no one cares about my feelings.

When I was a kid, I always wished
to be with my parents and be happy.
Now that I have them, I don't want them here.
It's cruel, yes… but real.
I'm tired of lies, my life is sadly incomplete.

Who I am is thanks to me!
So wrong, yes… but so mine.

When I needed advice, I had no one who could guide me,
instead my guardian did what she wasn't supposed to.
She stole my childhood and destroyed my freedom.
She never taught me the correct way
and fear fueled my soul.
I was robbed and no one can return to me what I lost.

I'm what I am, perhaps a monster,
but I can't hide the scars left in my heart.
I was sweet and all I ever received was confinement,
that's how I ended up as this strong and mean monster.

Deep inside of me, there's still a good person,
but I'm not sure if it's too late to start all over.

What I know is that I haven't yet found it,
the happiness I've always looked for.

I want to keep this secret to myself,
but it burns and kills my heart as I keep it in my chest.

I want to scream it but I can't,
my pride is too strong and I can't control it.

Someday, someone might read this.
This poem could cause the reader to cry,
perhaps, no one will get to read it
and to me it is the same thing.

It's enough just to write it in here,
where you, the reader, can see,
my life point of view and what do I think.

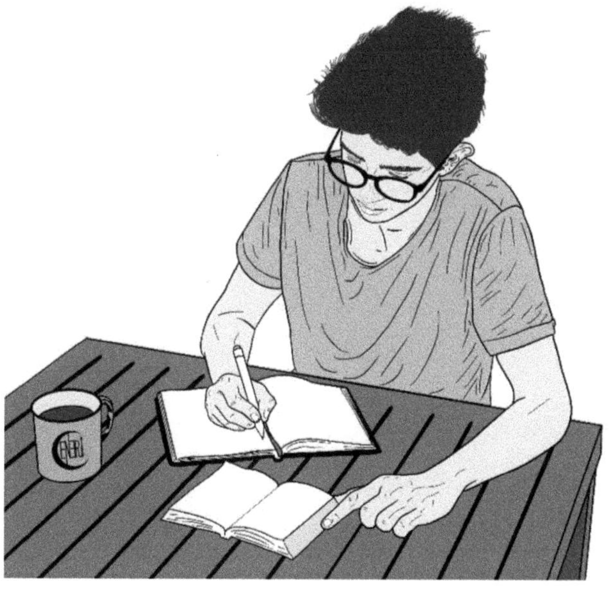

BLACK ROSES

Black roses:
Dead, pain and loneliness.
Sadness, crying and darkness.
Dark secrets and a bleeding heart.

Black roses:
Mean identities behind masks.
Defeated and weakened.
Blood, tears, and eternal pain.

Black roses:
Evil sight and devilish.
Sins and massacres waiting to happen.
The wish of instant death.

Black roses:
Black magic and death wakes from the sleep.

Black roses:
To my father who made me like this.
Dark life, scary smiles and chilling laughter.
The ones you sent and left on my door.

Black roses:
You're the reason I'm still in this world.

I CAN'T LET YOU HAVE ME

I'm sick of trying.
I can't let you have me.

This is not a game.
It's the maze of liars.

I'm just sick of crying.
It can't be the same.

I can't let you have me,
not whenever you want me.

Please just walk away.
I prefer it this way.

Please leave, don't stay.
I can hear you laughing.

You never loved me,
this was just a waste of time.
Please leave me, don't look behind.

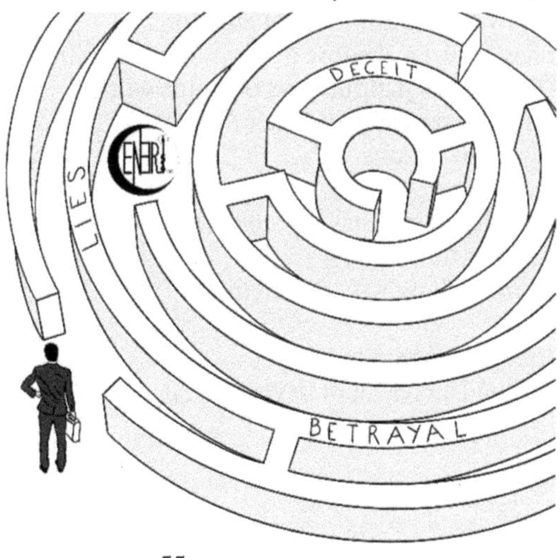

DARKNESS OF THE FORGOTTEN

I'm starting to lose my mind,
it claims something impossible to have.
My soul wants to sell itself,
it says that I'm not worthy to have its faith.
My sad eyes cry as they see,
that my mind doesn't want to obey me.

The shiny moon sings sadly,
as the day begins,
because its journey ends
when the sun comes out again.
The bright sun angrily rules over earth,
burning everything
until there's nothing but ash.
People have forgotten how beautiful life is,
and sadly,
they let themselves fall down until they die.
They make their own graves,
an extinction that happened yesterday,
something close to it will occur again.

Life was beautiful but not anymore,
today is just a shadow that, without light, life is lost.
The seas are painful deserts in this world,
not understandable words of verses,
rhymes with tone.

Now the silence has my voice,
it makes this a hell
where nothing's worth anything.

I have no reason to be,
the good angel I will never be.

Blood on my hands
means I did something wrong,
now my conscience won't leave me alone.

There is no time or space to stay,
I leave, goodbye there's nothing else…

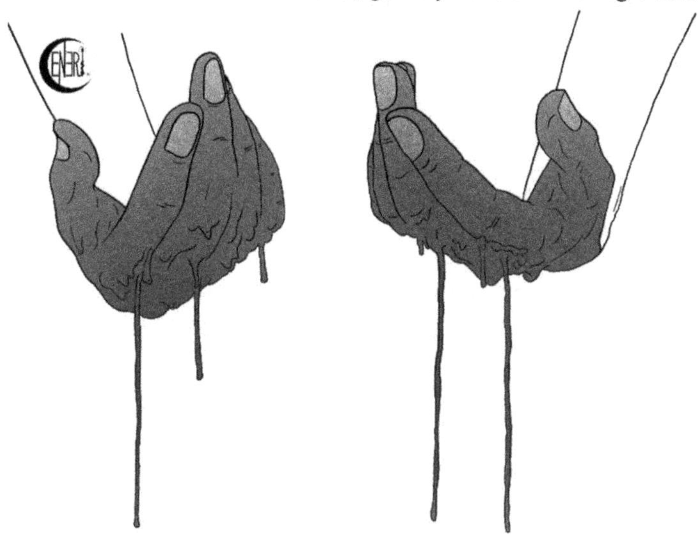

THE DIVISION

Human's division is my case and truth.
It's the dark and the light,
these are the lines of a rhyme.

Every time I remember you,
I do not know what to think.
If I hate you or love you,
if it's rain or my tears.
How can I forget about you,
if I never knew there was an end?
What can I do if I'm blind?
Today, for you, I just want to fly.

I want to walk over the clouds
and fly under the sea.
I wish to find a pearl without a name,
and engrave yours on it forever.
I feel that today, we are no longer together,
although you will always be in my heart.
Tell me how not to love you so much?
If you're me and I'm your other half.

It's the human's confusion
and a double personality.
It's the good and the bad,
it's life's option on our chosen paths.

Today, I started to cremate your memories.
Today, I prefer to hate you,
to think you're no longer in my way.

Today, I want to forget you
and you have no clue how badly.
From the depths of my heart,
I bury you in this deep ocean.

Today, I walk over fire
and sleep with the nightmares.
Today that skull I founded,
Today, as I see of you, only ashes remained.
I feel the deepest pain,
as I see I loved you
and now you are no more than waste.
As I see yesterday and our old love,
as I see this day and our dark road.

I feel that this is an ugly nightmare.
But you left without giving me a farewell.
This is just one more pain, a love with no merge.

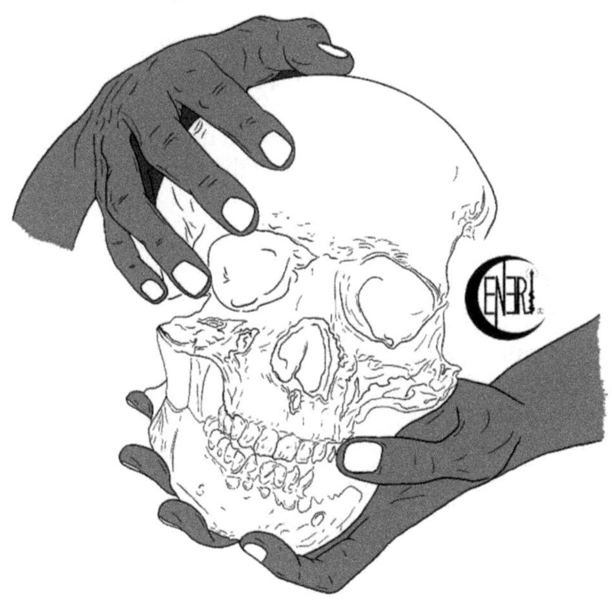

VANISH WISH

The years go by as leaves
fly between the winter's wind.
Year after year, I believe in myself.
But as soon as winter comes near,
my heart gets broken and I lose my strength.

Time always leaves,
it never waits for our dreams.
It's impossible to surpass time…
but I prefer to risk it all.
Every time I think memories went away.
I feel afraid. I feel panic to walk away,
panic to not come back.

I have lost the will to be what I once wished,
traveling long distances, just to see you once again.

I want to forget everything you've done to me.
I wish I could pretend nothing happened between us.

I just wish to hug you and have you in my arms,
just to love you without thinking of the past.

You have left my soul torn apart,
murmuring what could I have done.

You might have taken death away,
but you will die no matter what you do to stay.
You're beyond evil as much as you can comprehend,
you've destroyed everything beneath you.
What should I get for staying with you?
Other than losing my head.

It could be awesome to have you here,
to revert time and have you at my feet.
To create a world, where lies and pleasure rule my soul.

To believe that I didn't lose you, to be sure I did choose you.
I don't believe in coincidences, and your time is over.

The ugly reality in this world is the only existing thing.
If I pretend that I like you, it doesn't mean it's real.

Masters and slaves, are now far away.
It's us attracted like magnets.

I feel sorry for you,
my heart without you is complete.
All we were once is lost. Don't whine about it,
our story is over and I have to go.

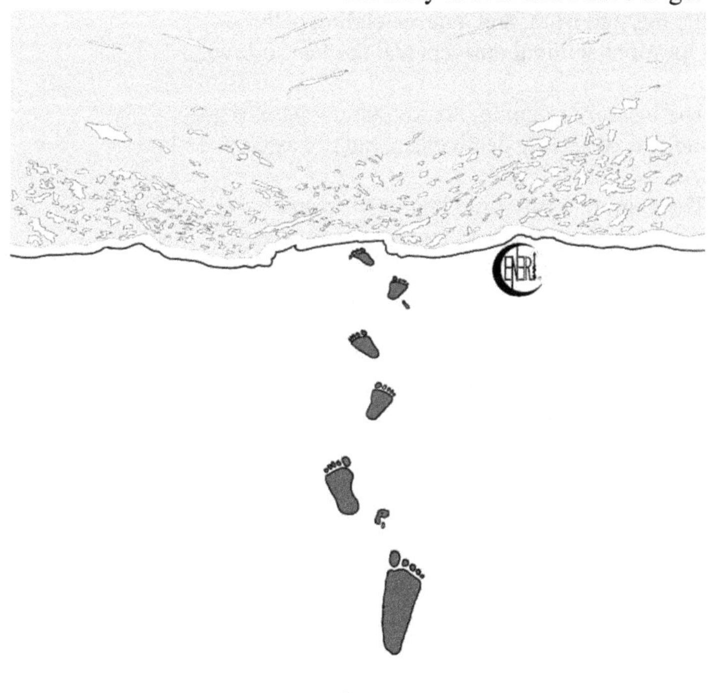

THE TURN

Today, I'm a person prepared to die in loneliness.
Yesterday, I was nobody.
Today, I'm more than what I want to be.
Today, my goals ran away from me.
Yesterday, I wanted to be someone. Today, I'm by myself.

In moments like this one you are no longer with me.
Now is when the revolution begins.
I have no reason to be a poet anymore,
nor to suppress the pain of my wounds.

I have too many doubts, with the fear of failing.
The moon, stars, the sea, and its sand,
the desert and the sun, the pain inside of my heart.
One adventure and the will to cry,
the lies and truth, and a never-ending path.
Questions without answers and the fear to love.

The insanity reigning, not knowing where to go,
the fear of feeling death close, but not as close as love.

The shining of my light begins to return.
The night escapes and loneliness walk away.
There is no more torture, no more tears,
sadness is gone – freedom is on its way.

Today, my soul is not happy at all.
The sky shines and burns me.
My soul cries for your love, love that wasn't worth it.
The book opens,
and a new chapter of illusion begins.

I have too many doubts, with the will to overcome.
It's the lines of a poem;
pure and sincere love written in rhymes.

The pain leaves… it hurts less as I see you fade away.
The extreme adventures… with the will to enjoy and feel.
To let the lies, walk away, to finally see its end.
The answers come back and my pains disappear.

The mental hospital collapses and I start a trip without an ending
point. Death snares me, but because of fear, I'm not going to be
in loneliness.

Someday I will leave… I am ready to go to that place, but I will
live every other day as if tomorrow was the end, as if I will
never return, and one day, it will become truth.

I will show my love to the people who love me, not to want one
more day. I don't want to know what I can achieve. What I'm
today, tomorrow I will no longer be.

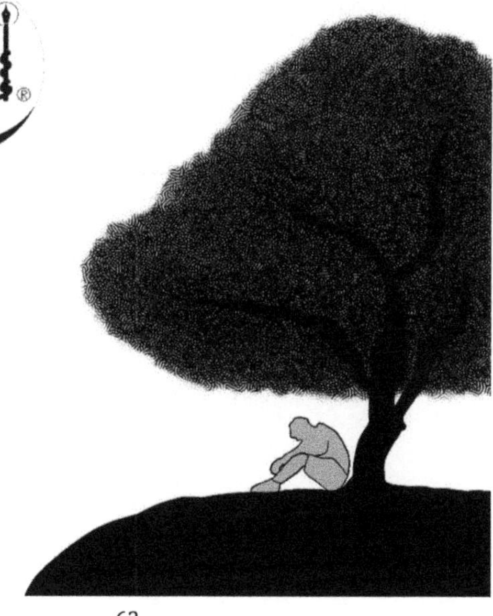

THE POETRY OF MY HEART

No one ever has crossed the divine line.
Don't you let it close your eyes!
Keep it close to the dark, so it won't be the last time.

I have tears in my heart,
tearing my whole self apart.
I had family, but that was a long time ago.
I was theirs and they were mine.

Close to me, there is no sign.
I haven't left, I still feel bad.

I could have saved them, but I can't now.
I wonder why I doubted it.

I stood there and let them die.
I can't believe I didn't cry;
horrible and cruel is what I was,
not a single remorse for such a night.

I've felt no remorse that night.
As a human I can't believe I was incredibly harsh.
No one ever had such a grim mind.
No one ever felt so afraid to die,
as I feel now for my life.

DON'T JUDGE ME

I don't want to think about it anymore,
I just want to get away from the world.

My broken dreams I don't want to see any longer,
I just want to fly from one planet to another.

What I do and what I did,
that shouldn't concern anyone,
if you're not supporting me please remain silent.
I'm not perfect, I'm not great,
but I have rights
so, don't tear your hearts with envy.

By hating me, you only make me stronger,
I am bad, and no, I never leave anyone wounded
when I start something, I always finish it.
I don't lie to you, I never leave anyone alive,
my victims to the graveyard
and I keep accumulating crimes.

For a good salary a murderer I have become,
I am what you see... with the most original of styles.
It is me, the God of my own destiny.

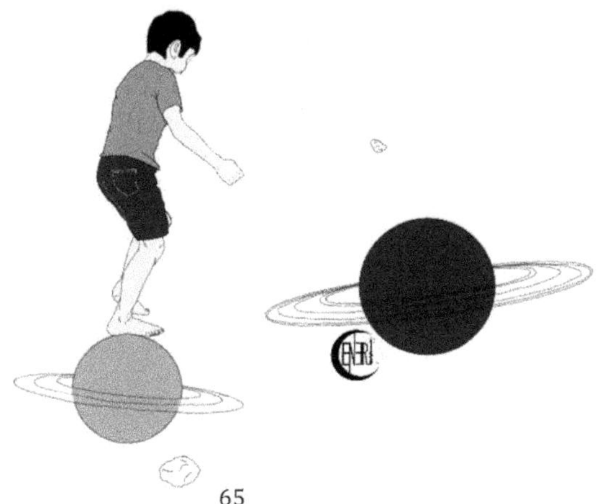

ONE LAST WRITTEN WISH

I have here, one last written wish.
I want the dead to revive,
and the living to die at last.

I want the moon to disappear,
and the sun to explode in your name.
I want the sea to come out,
and the lightning to fall on me.

I want to see people screaming,
thinking that everyone is going to die.
To enjoy their phobia and their fears,
to feel that I am the only one with courage.

I want to see everyone fall around me,
and be the only one that didn't fall.
Fear is a mental prison,
I don't have time for weaknesses.

Don't cry, or scream, I have no mercy anymore,
I hate being weak but I have hope in God.
I can't feel sad for anyone,
if I can't feel sorry for myself.
The world keeps moving and nobody is ever happy,
live life, that the end is near.

YOUR LOVING'S WORTH

I want to tell you so badly, I love you!
but wanting to say it isn't truly saying it.

I wish you were sincere,
but you look like an actor as you always read off a script.

I wish I had a heart of steel,
to not feel your contempt.

Those pains and tears that I still feel,
the sufferings that run through my veins,
are consuming me slowly.

Today I swear, I prefer to see you leave,
to see you get away from me.

I prefer a thousand times to let go an 'I love you',
than to pay with my life,
for an impulse that my heart can't control.

How could I not prefer to live my life?
I can't exchange it for a selfish person like you,
I can't let my life go to waste with you,
you're not worth making that mistake.

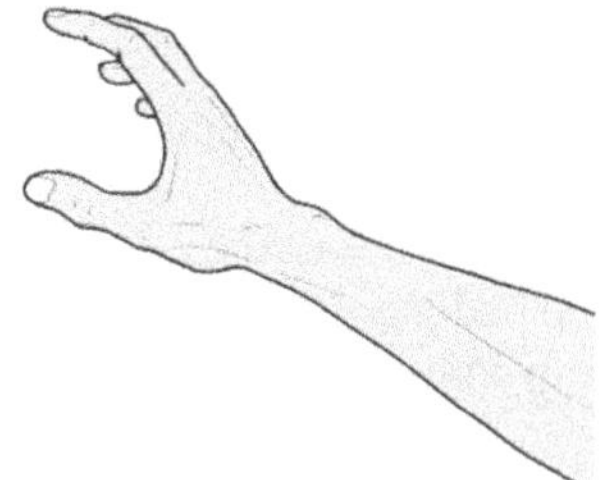

DARK ANGEL

It's past six o'clock, every time the sunset appears,
love hurts more as the memories fade,
the memories that caused pain,
feelings that the heart doesn't understand.

An illusion, it gets lost in confusion,
between lives resigned to death.
I can't go to war without a shotgun,
nor without enough tools to end the enemy head on.
I can't throw myself into the ocean,
not without knowing how to swim against the current.

I can't try to fly without wings,
much less govern a place where nothing exists.
I don't admit that I still feel fear, why should I?
It's our disguises what set us apart,
to be ourselves, is to take away our strength,
to be no more than unbelievers and fabricators.

Everyone in life has a good side,
what I was yesterday, today I don't want to be again,
I get more being who I am, than by being a pathetic bastard.

I have decided to be forever the black angel,
who has no mercy,
not even for those who brought me to this world,
who loves darkness and the calm in it,
who despite thinking about the future, thinks of what was?
The accumulated hatred does not kill, it gives hope...
it helps me thrive...
and with my head held high.

Someday I will die... lost in an abyss I will stay,
the bad guys don't have happy endings,
they either end up in jail or death without crime.

TODAY

Once again, the sky is gray, raindrops on my face fall. Lightning
flashes fall repeatedly, disturbing the silence of the city. The
birds cry and fly away, they travel aimlessly lost
in the dark.

I would like to help them and illuminate their journey,
they fly away crying, hell is where they are headed to.
My happy songs went to oblivion, and never made it back,
today I remember old friends, today that I'm alone.

Today the sky is broken, and the end is getting closer,
today I know that I am a child who never had his mother.
The clock of my heart stops to meditate,
for seconds I stay between this world and the other side.

Feeling my fears and the balance of the truth,
feeling the pain of not having been someone else.
My cell phone and a pen as I sit in class,
with my notebook on this armchair as I cry,
looking at the gray classroom windows.

Gloria Trevi and her song "Un día más",
the train, the window and her life
seem pathetic, but not as much as my own life.

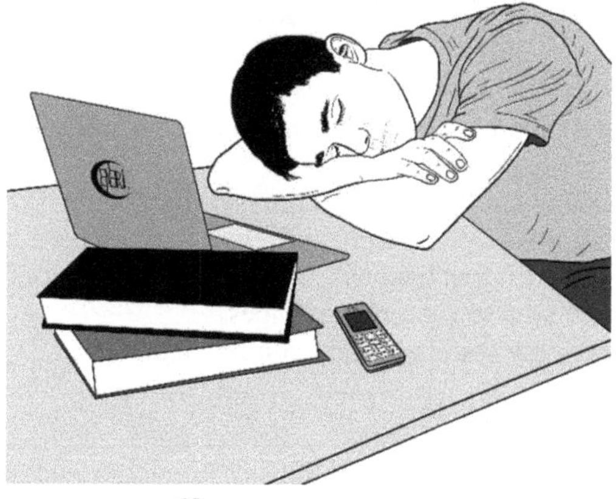

LIFE CONSEQUENCES

Hate and love are similar feelings,
very different and equal at the same time.
Hate, the feeling of the darkest hell.
Love, the pure feeling of faith itself.

The two are very different,
although they come from the same source.
I believe and I will always believe that surely
It's the connection of the heart and the mind.
The mind commands and the heart obey.
Hate is always provoked,
instead, love is almost always rejected.
That is why I chose the path of hatred,
and not the path of love...
Love caused me so much pain,
pain that turned into hatred and resentment...
Hate and resentment that will be in my heart
from today until the day I die.

Because many people think that life
is what we hold in our minds,
but my opinion is very different,
even if there are probabilities that it may not be true.

The only thing that I understand today is my life and reality,
and even if I don't want to accept it, one day I will have to,
because that's my destiny and I will have to stop fighting it,
to live in the now, so I don't have to think about my end...

Meanwhile I will distract myself by having fun,
that way, I won't think of hell, where I'll burn in the end.
And until that happens, I will have a little more fun,
making a few cunning choices,
since my soul is already condemned.

CHAPTER 4

INSECURITIES

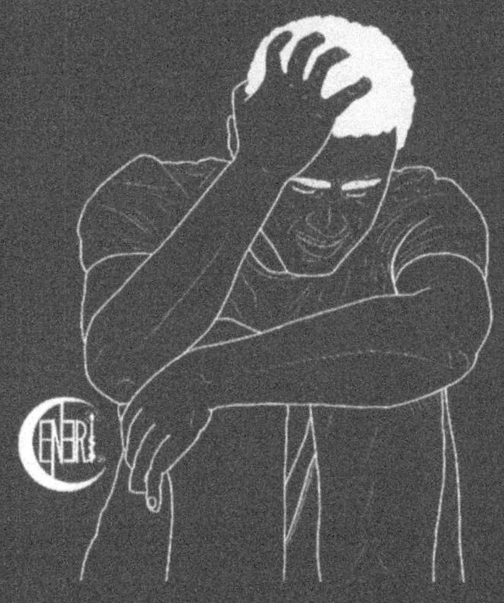

MY PHOBIAS

There were days, many difficult mornings,
that I lost my strength. I felt tired, abandoned and hopeless.

It's hard for me to keep standing,
to keep waiting for the future to come and take me.
Sincerely, I can be strong,
but not strong enough to avoid memories.
They hurt as hope fades away.

I feel like a bird that wants to fly.
I don't feel sure, so I stop.
I stayed in solitude waiting for a try.
Trying to get out of hell, I fall.
I can't find myself; I lost my sight.
There is no way for me to get out of here.
I have one chance to face my fear.
Upon it, my heart was afraid of me.

I have thought about me and my future.
I have never been sure of anything.
I think of something; I believe in a different thing.
I hear other things, and I see no way out of here.
My life isn't easy; I'm afraid of being ignorant.

I'm afraid of not being accepted by the Lord as everybody
rejected my love. I'm the abandoned human lost in war. Like a
grain of sand lost in the desert, like a gaze lost between the stars,
and the sound that faded in the silence.

I wish to scream but I fear no one would hear.
I'm sick of fighting against fear. I'm tired of living in this cruel
world. I'm tired and I can't smile to the Lord.

I'm not happy and I can't do anything.
I'm dying of fear. I'm afraid to show what I feel.

SLEEP FAITH

It was no more than a weird dream.
I saw you dead, and you looked at me.
It wasn't life, it was my fear.
I wanted you, but you wanted to leave.

I'm here right now, I'm falling down.
I'll be right here until the end of time.
It doesn't matter if what I'm doing isn't right!
I don't care – I love you and you own my heart.

I have no choice, but to wait for you to come back.
Who cares if I waste my whole life?
If you're not here, life has no meaning.
I should've left you years ago,
now it's too late for me to go.

I have no other choice but to be your lover.
Please come back, I need you so badly.
I can't breathe and it's hard to die.

I wish I could decide;
I wish you were here under the endless sky.
I want you to be my love and me your spouse.
I want you here; can you please look through my eyes?

I'm dying for you but you went to the other side of the wall.
I can't cross it – it's too high.

I'm in the darkness while you're in paradise.
I'm dying for your love, don't walk away.
Please don't ignore me, I will fade away.
Save me now, now that you can.

Don't come back tomorrow – it will be too late.

SOUL FEAR

I haven't seen you, but you're always in my mind.

I'm losing the hope to be with you,
I'm feeling lost in this life.

I'm afraid of your decision, afraid to let go.
I still don't have you,
I don't know what's wrong.

My soul demands your love, but it seems you're lost.

If I could, I'd clear your doubts,
let you know you are my world.

Your ominous eyes scream at me,
I ask, "What's the big deal?"
All they answer is, "It's not a dream."

I wish I could be part of your dreams.
Share my deep secrets and make you feel
that you can always count on me.

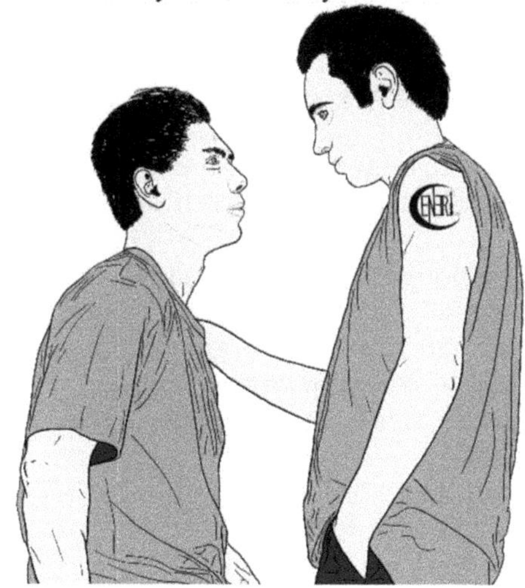

HOPE

Days keep passing by; people come and go,
just as I keep changing and losing my mind.

I'm here… lonely in solitude,
listening to the deep and dark soul's pain,
sins and sorrows created by men.
I see those tears in your eyes,
but I can't do anything – you are far away.

I feel how time moves away, I am afraid this is not the same.
As I remember your face,
your hair, and your beautiful smile.
I swear I hear your voice, but you're gone.
Maybe these are no more than just lines,
painful words for the love of mine.

Could it be that one day you will return,
to have you here with me and love you?
Could it be that I will find you as time pass by?

I ask myself too many questions that keep damaging me.
It's poison to think you're not here,
to see you went away from me.
When I loved you the most, you just left me here and lost.

It's hard to live in a world full of lies,
and sometimes I feel myself suicidal.

I'm lost, come back to my arms.
It doesn't have to be right now, but the sooner… the better.
Why did you run away from this town?
Don't hide your problems for later,
just get rid of them before it's too late.

MISTAKES

I used to have a smile, but it went away.

I used to be so peaceful, and now everything's destroyed.

Right now, I'm so wild, and careless.

Right now, I'm unfaithful, and I'm just having fun.

I used to like writing, but I think my writing sucks.

I used to like the darkness, and I still like its cold.

I might be the worst, I might do everything wrong,
I might have no control,
but I'm still human, I'm still a person.

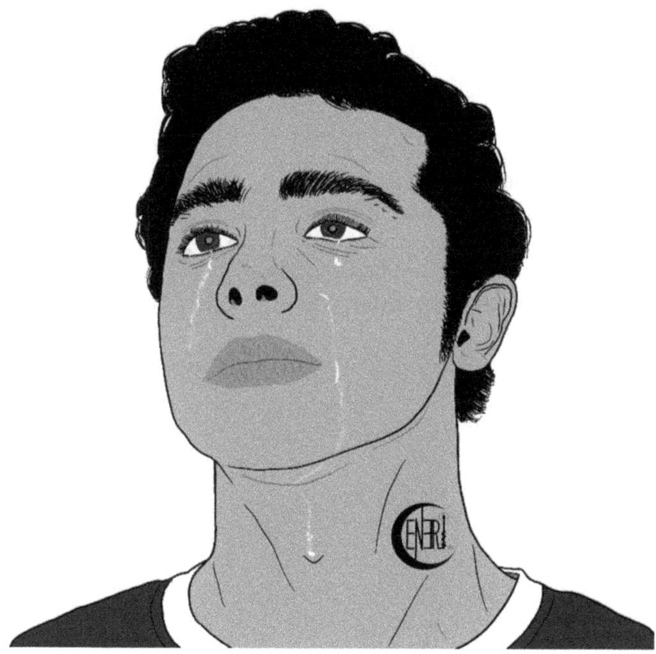

WHAT COULD I SAY, BUT TO...

Sometimes, I wish to fade away,
but fading away doesn't solve anything.
I wish not to hear you say
what you told me, without thinking it though.

I wish I could run far, far away,
where I could feel secure and not hated.
I don't know what to believe nowadays!
There are many versions and many paths...
Who knows which one is the right one?

Time doesn't completely heal our wounds,
but it does make us forget about our pain for a while.
Who we were, who we are and who will we become...!

It's something unreal,
but it's there, although it's invisible,
it's the terror hidden behind mirrors,
it's a deep cold feeling.

I don't have much left to say,
only to say I am no longer who I was!
Nowhere to go, but where life takes us!

Who to listen to, who to blame for love?
Who can hear me in my room with my sorrows?
I just don't know.
I'm confused; I need time to organize my mind.

I need money, I need time, I need things, and I need my life.
I don't want things; I hate to be out of my mind.
I wish not to say this, I wish to keep it in my heart.
I'm just waiting here,
waiting for an absolution which won't come.

I'm pathetic, I'm crying over you.
I'm an idiot crying because I lied.

I still can remember, our love I couldn't trust,
I slept over the water under the moonshine light.
I could've saved myself across your eyes,
but Lucifer took me without answering me – why?
It's cruel, but I need to come back to life,
I need someone to save me,
to love me and hold my arm.

I have always been too selfish,
but I believe I deserve a second chance.
My eyes seem to be looking,
looking for your sweet heart.
Come and save me before the end of times.

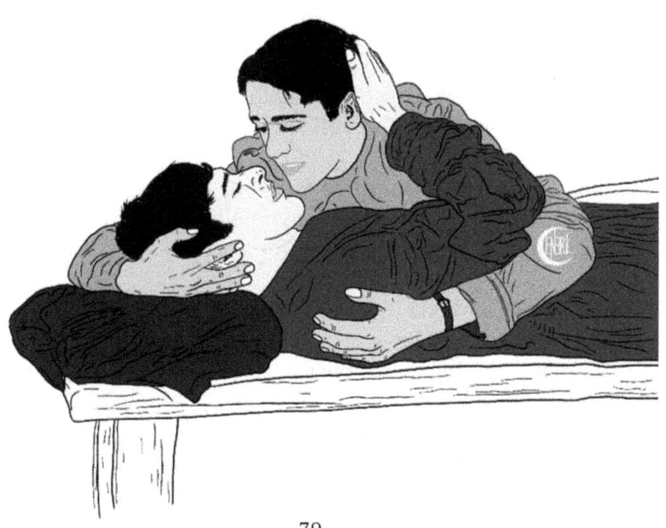

LIES

I thought that by staying in this world,
nothing would happen, but peace and love.
Finally, when one door opens,
the next two are closed.

I think and think… but I really can't figure it out.

I wish to believe that this is a mistake,
that nothing is wrong with me.
I feel empty, incomplete… But it's always been like this.
I was so busy helping others.
Meanwhile… my life was at its end.

There's no light at the end of life,
and I'm afraid to not find my answers.
Loneliness has been always my shelter,
and misfortune one of my favorite desserts.

This could be destiny, but it's too hard for me to understand,
I can't keep living behind this mask,
this infinite pain marked in my heart.

I can't keep laughing nor crying for my life.
Everything happens because of something,
and because of someone I'm still empty.

Now I have two very clear options
either to watch you all die or to let you all do the same.
I'm sure I'm good, but not enough for anyone.

I'm feeling sad for myself… but I can't wait for miracles.
The sky is starry and I have no more tears to cry.
My eyes have blinded themselves,
all I see is darkness tonight,
a dark shadow from hell, a human's lie…
a person who lied to himself, that someone was me.

I MISS YOU

I'm excited… although I still don't know why.
I seem to be falling in love, love has returned to me.

It's the best thing happening to me,
something I don't want to private myself from.
I turn to the mirror only to see that you're not really here,
I feel deeply enraged and I just want to scream.

I don't want to miss you, but I can't get you out of my mind.
I covered myself in black ink and I threw myself to the sea,
you can't imagine my regret; I'll never see you again.

The story of my life wasn't special,
in spite of that I still think
that life with you would've been something incredible.

I wish I could be alive, to see you breathe,
hear you say all those things, that you never said.

To feel you beside me, and not let you escape,
to adore you, to love you and have you for eternity.

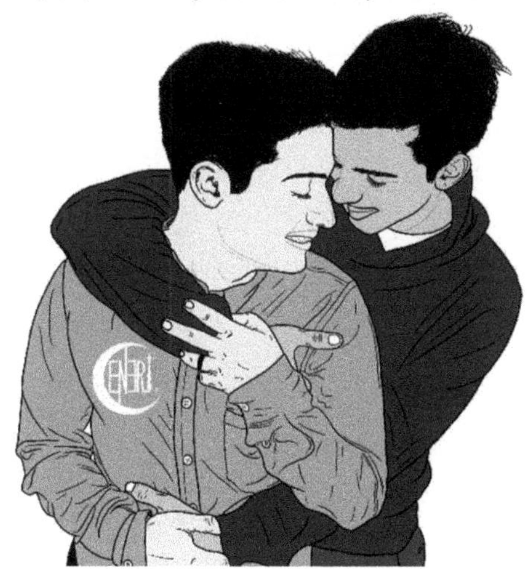

QUESTIONS

How do I finish a story that never started?
What can I do to have love?
How can I love someone,
if no one offers me their arms?

What can I do to make someone
take pity on my pain?
How can I order my mind
to not be confused?

Why does nobody value who I am?
How can I cry for something
without logic or reason?

I want to give myself to somebody
without fearing getting hurt!
How can I choose you
if I can't even choose what's right for me?

I want to get lost with you,
only thinking of being alone together one day.

How can I rip my heart out
to avoid feeling this burning love?
I want you to heal me
and love me for who I am.

How do I amend these errors
that apart me from a better world?
How can I not cry while discovering who I am?
Discovering I was someone who was taken advantage of.
Someone who's half of a whole!

With this poem I ask for a tiny wish.
May you come to me
and be what nobody has ever been before.
If you give me the opportunity, I can love you
and give you the paradise you deserve.
To make of us, a union of love and forget about our past,
to be as good or better than a beautiful and lovely sunrise,
to be more than we always wanted to be.

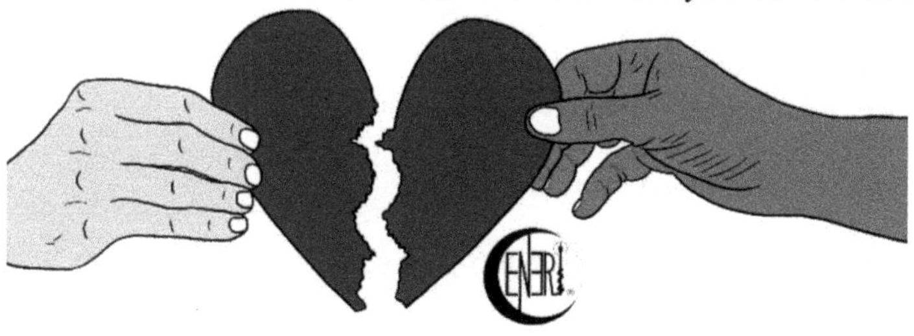

IMPOSSIBLE LOVE

I would like to understand you,
to let you go forever,
so that one day you could find someone
who can love you.

I doubt that he could love you
the way I love you,
I doubt that he could live only for you
despite of your pains.
I wish you the best, what you deserve, perhaps,
wishing him to love you
the way my heart feels love for you.
My soul doesn't accepts losing you,
but between cigarettes and alcohol,
I will take you out of my soul and mind.

Even if I have to get away from you,
I will...
in order to stop suffering next to your scorn,
your selfishness,
and your cold loneliness.
Anything is better...
than staying here,
I feel cornered in your absence
and I can't get out of here.

What could I do to make you love me?
My heart beats faster when I have you near.

I don't know what to do with my life,
I can't find answers or clues,
I don't want to keep looking for something,
that I probably won't find.

I have a fatigue soul and weary feet, that got old as days passed.
I love you! —Who cares? If it's me you forget,
if it's me you don't tell what you're doing
and what your plans are?

I don't ask to know everything, only what's necessary,
there is no time, it's late to start all over again,
I have no energy left, much less the will to try,
goodbye impossible human,
you're nothing more than a saved memory.

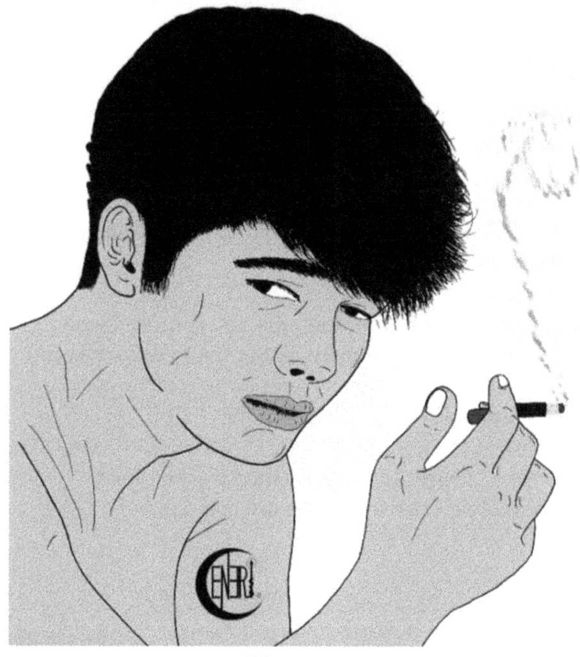

WHAT SHOULD I DO?

Today I don't know whether to continue or to stop!
I wish I could pause my life before taking my last breath,
to feel for a second my undying fear to a cold death.

I wonder what will happen if I let my life take its course.
And if I die now will I be preventing more pain?
How can I continue living life without having a little faith?

I sometimes feel that a bottle of pills, would be best...
A drug that could heal my pain.

I don't see how I could continue,
yesterday I didn't know anything,
today a human touched me,
he took me by force, he caused pain to my body and soul.

Who could imagine it?
What a great harm, a shameless crime!

I suffer now as I struggle with this great depression,
I don't understand who I am or where to go.

I wish someone could understand me.
Why is it, that everyone lives between appearances?
Why the hell don't they see?

I feel that taking my life will only cause more damage,
endless nights of nightmares, under the pillows where I cry.
Maybe if I cut my wrists
in a bath tub and I let my blood pour.
A cold metal razor,
answers my desires that were killed by the rapist,
who doesn't deserve to live on my account.

OBSESSION

Loving in silence has its advantages,
nobody hurts you and you watch who you love.

The tears shed and the bitter moments,
they always take our time away.
They hurt our hearts, for one reason or another.

To think that you have him with you,
at your side ... That he kisses you, caresses you,
he protects you; he spoils you,
takes care of you and only your welfare interests him.

You can see in him, interest,
you will be able to feel intense love for him,
just fantasy... the illusion of a heart.

Orders of a mind without reasoning,
just to believe that you can love someone,
without price or condition,
something that always ends in a terrible obsession.

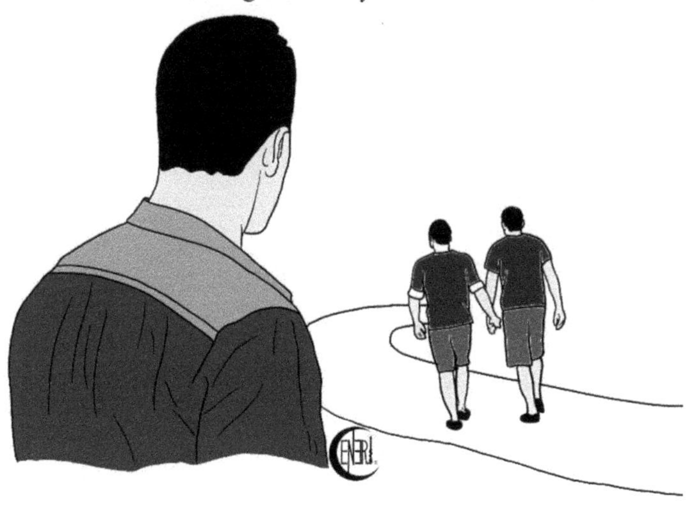

EMPHATIC EMPTINESS

It saddens me to remember those beautiful moments,
much sadder to remember that they are no longer with me,
my friends and classmates.

Sometimes I just want to be dead,
to draw a little attention,
to see what some people will do,
to observe what happens around me.

Other times I see the portraits,
pieces of our lives stored,
old moments that have passed,
and only in pictures have they been captured.

I would like to memorize more of those moments,
I want to feel happiness and torments,
I want everyone to remember being happy
and sad at the same time,
those adventures of happiness and sorrow.

I can see today that I'm not dead,
that this is just a script,
lines of writing that people with gestures,
will read, perhaps with disappointment.

The concept of this life,
are composed of photos and memories,
moments that we live day after day,
moments that freeze in time.

Today for example I want to cry,
today as I feel in me a resounding emptiness,
today that nothing comforts me,
today when I can't find the end to this world.

CHAPTER 5

PARTING

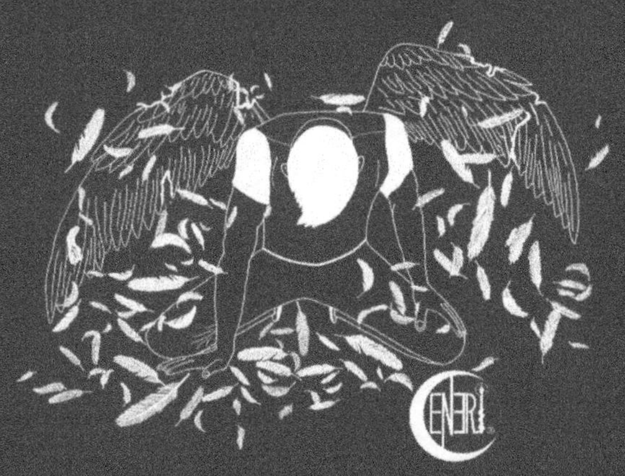

TIME TO GO

I feel ready, so let me go.
Don't try to stop me, don't…
it will not work!

It's time to leave here,
it's time for the wind to take me home.
I bet you'll miss me,
I promise it won't last long.

The snow calls me,
I can feel it through my bones.
I can't stop, all of me, is now gone.

I have a memory,
but it's getting lost,
it's lost in the darkness,
it's lost between my last hope.

Nightmares of allusions created by fear,
creations of a mind without memories,
souls of the past and painful words in my ears,
my mind is confused and doesn't know where it is.

Life's directions have consequences,
unfortunately, this is my punishment,
I leave now… as I am out of answers.

INCOMPLETE SINS

Nights dedicated to lovers in my youthful days,
hidden feelings in a motel bed,
cold illusions, over and over again.

We were hungry animals looking for meat,
no more than mirror reflections in the immense earth,
we did it…
because we wanted it.

It's always been the same thing,
dirty touching, sexy skin and pleasure,
naughty games from yesterday, now and always.

Paths beyond thoughts without sense
are the confusion that takes me away.
Suicide thoughts, drugs and alcohol end my faith.

Always alone… alone I will stay.
Who cares if I die right now,
tomorrow or in a decade?
It's the same thing, without cause,
there's no fear to fade away.

After long trips,
a promise to come back,
fear of death, trapped in time.
I happen to be dying,
lost in the screams of my cry.

Of myself, I left no marks,
all my ashes
are now part of the desert's sand.
I sleep among dreams,
between familiar faces that once were part of me.
I have now lost my way,
I lost my self and say.

Life's labyrinth is not as easy as we thought,
it's difficult to stay away from dreaming,
and that's how I end up in my tomb.

My eyes won't let me see you again,
and now I am on my way to Eden.

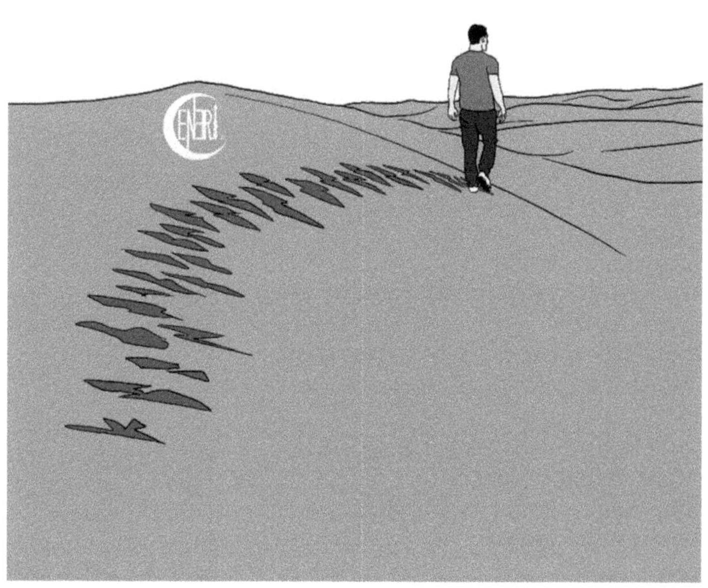

A TRIP WITHOUT RETURN

In my trip to this world,
the sky falls down as it sees my fears.
I don't want to turn to the mirror,
because I'm someone else I've never seen.

I'm tired of being manipulated.
I'm sick of pretending that I'm a good-mannered kid.
I'm a rebel and I can't pretend anymore.
I can't fake that I have no feelings; I do believe in love.

People criticize the way I talk, the way I dress and walk.
I want to escape and never turn back,
I'm tired of appearances; I can't be who I am.

Too many times, I have asked the Lord,
if someone loves me, because I see no one with me.
I wonder if there is someone alone,
so that way we could share our worlds.

I'd like to be remembered one day,
I don't want to die thinking I'll be forgotten.
I change my mind and many times,
I don't know what to do,
because I'm sensible and I fear to be hurt.

People talk about me, they just say trash,
I have never heard that someone loves me; I give up.

I believe it would be better to take off
and never come back.
I can't swim against the sea tides;
I'll let myself drown.

THE WISH IN YOUR ABSENCE

I am terrified of life because I don't know where you are.
I'm terrified to even open my eyes,
knowing that you are not here, by my side.

The shadow of your absence...
it's so cold without your presence.
I know I should not cling to you.
I know I will not always have you next to me,
but I can't accept to be without your essence.

Tell me what can I do to be able to live without you.
I want to be brave and just let you go...
I can't because I love you like I haven't loved in so long.
You are someone very special in my life,
you are illusion and light at every dawn, day after day,
but you aren't and never will be more than my friend.

I'll have to go, just like you will, one day,
we will walk separately and without looking back.
It's the best because although we wanted this, we know well,
that passionate love between us, it can never be.

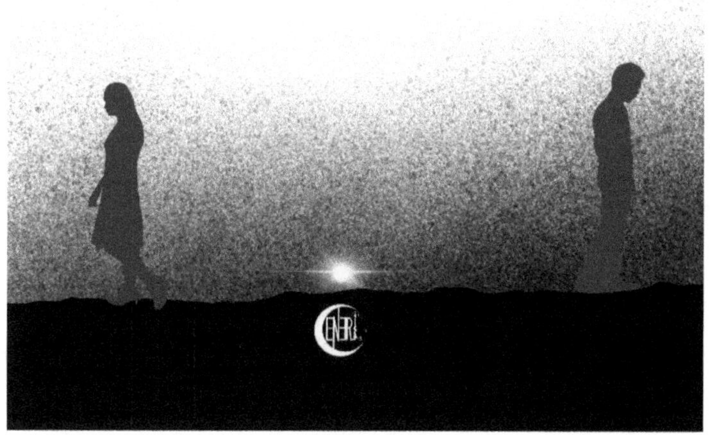

MY LAST LETTER

I can't promise you
anything when I leave,
I am not the one who
can make you happy.

I am so sad that I can't even smile,
so now I am going to hide for a while,
I am leaving without saying goodbye,
only to hide away my broken heart.

Having the deepest pain inside of my chest,
I can't contain my tears rolling down my face.
These are no more than forgotten lines
of an invisible love...
you were more
than everything someone could ever imagine,
you were my air,
my reasoning…
my all.

Now you are no more than a dream
lost in the edges of my mind.
You were the illusion I could've possibly been with,
but not anymore, it's too late to retry.

Forgive me if I wasn't what you expected of me.
Today I leave empty…
knowing you put an end to my feelings.
I'll save this memory in my mind,
to remind me
that I don't need someone like you in my life.

I'll now wake up from my dream,
to betray myself as fear kills my hope
and takes away my reasoning.
I now can only believe in the pain
that feeds my needs.

Today I'm not what I always planned to be!
These are the last lines I write for you,
today I give up all I ever had with you.

I'm going to become a new human
with a new life,
I'm taking with me
what I didn't share with you.

All things that yesterday you rejected…
all of what I tomorrow…
perhaps, will not be willing
to share with anyone.

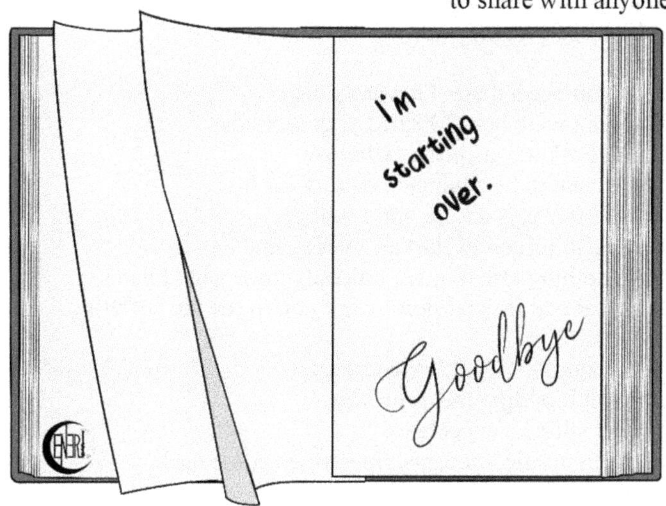

A THORNY FAREWELL

Once I had a dream, which hasn't come true yet.
Once I thought that perhaps someone could love me.

Today, I see I'm not what I always wanted to be.
My biggest fear has begun to turn into truth.
I'm accompanied but I still feel that I'm by myself.
I wish I could let myself die.
I wish to be cowardly enough to run away.
I don't want anything; I gave all of me.
I don't want to have enough strength to be alive.
I just want to leave and forget that I met all of you.
Pretend that I never existed.
Erase myself from this world and go far from here.

I ask myself, why wasn't I enough.
What else did you expect of me?
All I had; I gave to you.
God, please take me with you far from here.

When you needed me, I never said, no.
When you were hurt, I healed your wounds.
And all I asked was just a little love.
I don't want to be a human begging for love.
With this poem, I assure you I will go.
There is no reason to start all over again.
I have nothing else to give; I already gave what I had.
Now I have to leave, I don't want you to see me suffering.

By the hand of God, I leave today,
just to let him drop me as he sees,
I wasn't what he expected.
Today, in my final journey, memories come back,
I remember insults and hate.
I remember things I don't want to see again.
It's not possible not to feel the pain of my heart.

I asked myself; what did I do wrong?
But the truth is that I have never been special.
Actually, I am worth less than anyone.

I don't want to see nor think I'm leaving.
But I have to do it and there is no turning point.

Today, I am writing,
my tears fall and nothing can stop them.
I can't stop the crying nor my sour loneliness.
What I gave wasn't enough and everyone made me cry.

I can't see what's coming next.
All of you took my sight away and left me in the darkness.
I'm walking alone with my destiny and by the hand of God.

Today, I'm leaving
—yesterday, my love, you didn't appreciate.
Perhaps, tomorrow when you learn to appreciate me,
I'll come back.
But I don't assure you anything;
today I leave with a broken heart as I'm falling apart.

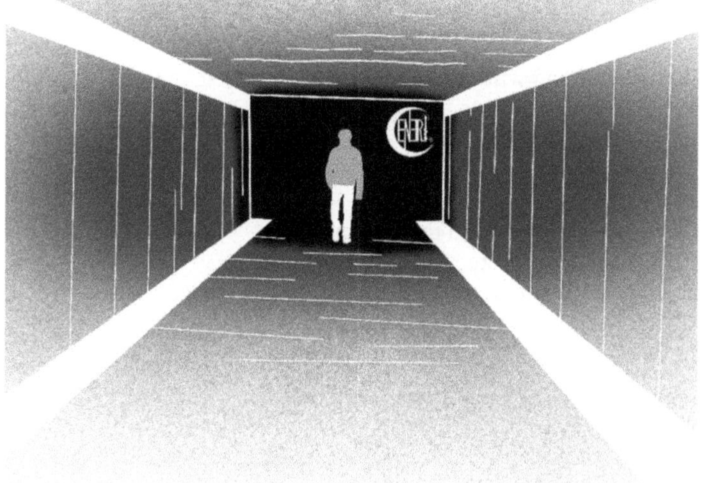

ANOTHER PAINFUL FAREWELL

I want to expand my wings,
to start my last trip.
I want to believe no one needs me anymore,
so that way,
I can feel free to go.

After this trip,
I don't promise to come back.
This is the end of my journey,
a painful farewell which won't hold me back.

It's time for me to leave;
it's time for me to fly.
I'm a rebel and a cynic;
I'm who I want to be.
I was lovely and obedient;
someone who you'll never see again.

It's the farewell to my friends,
friends I don't want to abandon.
But I have to move on,
there's no way to stop what will come.

Time leaves and with it,
my way out gets closer.
It's the cry and the laugh,
from too many friends who I have left behind.

These are the letters and the memoirs,
the ones I'll always keep in my heart.
It's time to fly away, today I leave one more town.

A new adventure
and the willingness to overcome,
new friends and problems to battle.
Beautiful dreams that turn true,
it's for my own good,
let me go.

Although I won't come back,
I will keep you in my mind,
in the deepness of my heart,
as something special.

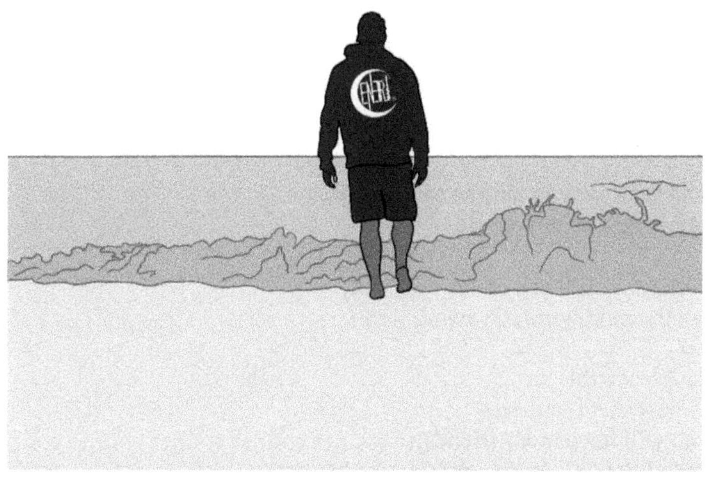

I have nothing else to give
nor have I more surprises to show.

I was wrong and boring
but it was for society.

I feared to see the mirror
to avoid breaking its reflection.

It's the farewell
to the beloved people,
whom I wish not to leave behind.

But it's time for me to be gone,
time comes – it leaves,
it never stays and always goes.

The same way I came in to your life,
someone else will come.

Perhaps you'll cry on my way out,
but the pain will fade away.

As I leave this day,
I know that tomorrow
you will have more friends,
and although it hurts my heart – goodbye,
I can't turn around.

VERSES
OF
PAIN

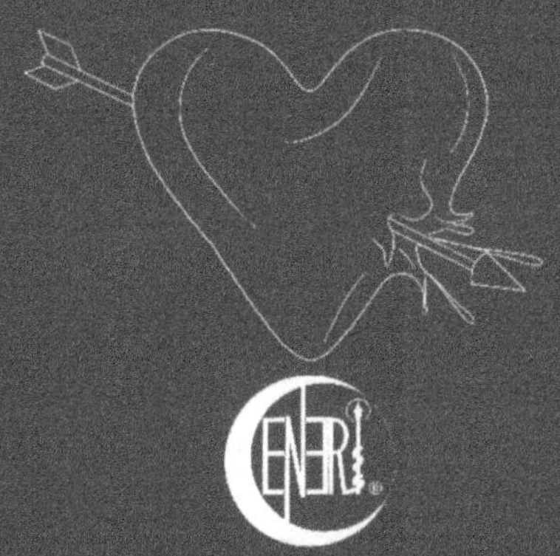

How much more time I have to cry?
How much more time I need to be quiet?
I can't face this true that keeps me broken,
sorrows keep me away from awaking…

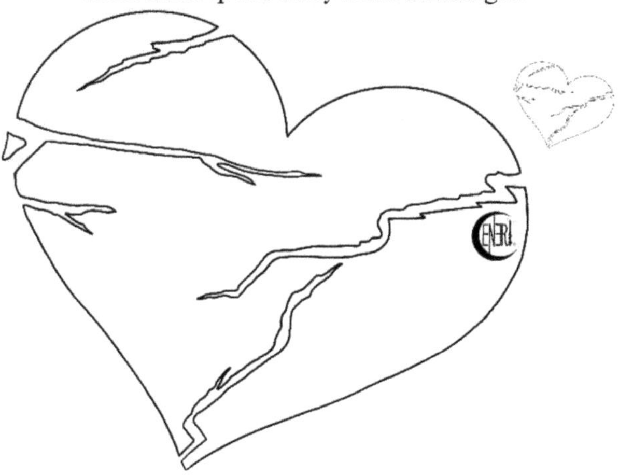

Sometimes I want to fly,
but I don't have wings to try.
sometimes I want to cry,
but I don't have tears to try.
and as I know that you could never be in my arms,
my soul feels sad,
sad to know that you have someone in your life,
it makes me run away still loving you so much.

If you want to come back, please don't even think about it.
I am not in here and if you come, all you'll ever see
are remains of my life and questions
like "How?" and "Why?",
you left me here and alone with all of my love…

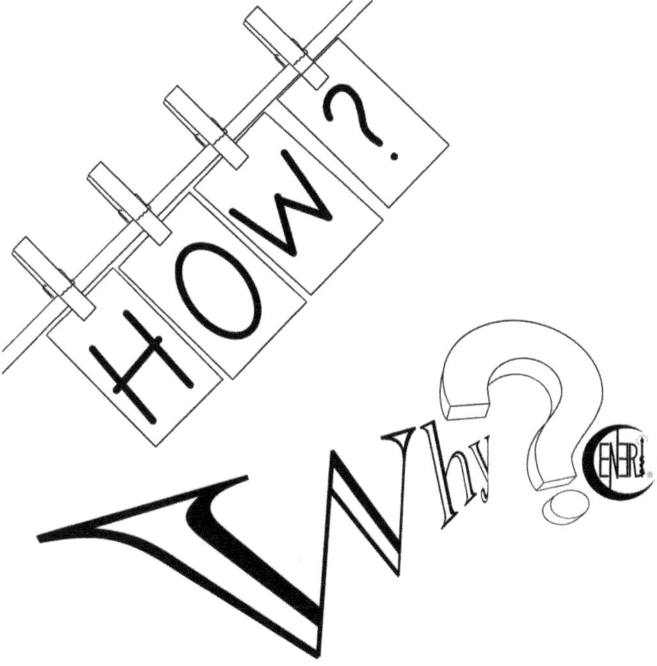

I don't want to be in here because the pain hurts me.
Sometimes I want to scream
but I fear nobody would hear me.
And only the death can take me
-until the hell and kill me,
because of suffer I have no needs
and no one can understand me.
No one feels this pain that now is hurting my heart,
and it's trying to get rid of me,
ripping my whole self apart…

I'm so closer to my end, and I don't know why and when?
I only know that is not fair and it doesn't heal my pain.
I feel more to give up than keep trying,
because I am really tired.
As the storm hits with its rain,
it makes me feel ready to care less,
to die right now or to live through this stress.

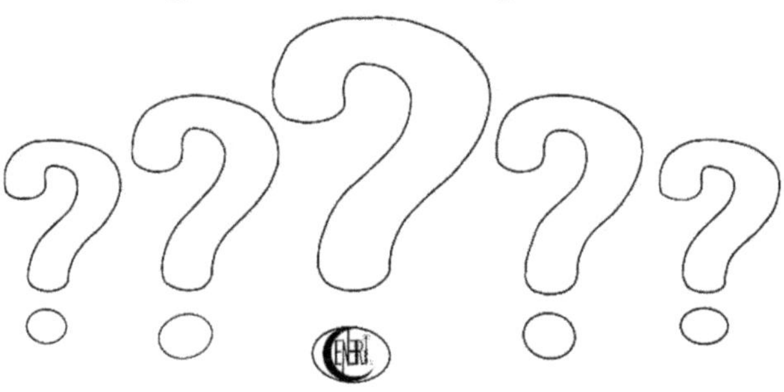

I don't want to cry please don't lie…
You will not be right because you won't be all mine.
I don't know why sometimes you don't want to try.
Seems you don't care about it
and now I only want to die,
because I don't need this life
if you're not going to come back.

It's so painful to remember the past of my life,
now I don't have time to tell, something that was…
I now have to shut up because someone don't want,
he doesn't want me to tell you about back in time,
about what happen in nineteen ninety-nine…

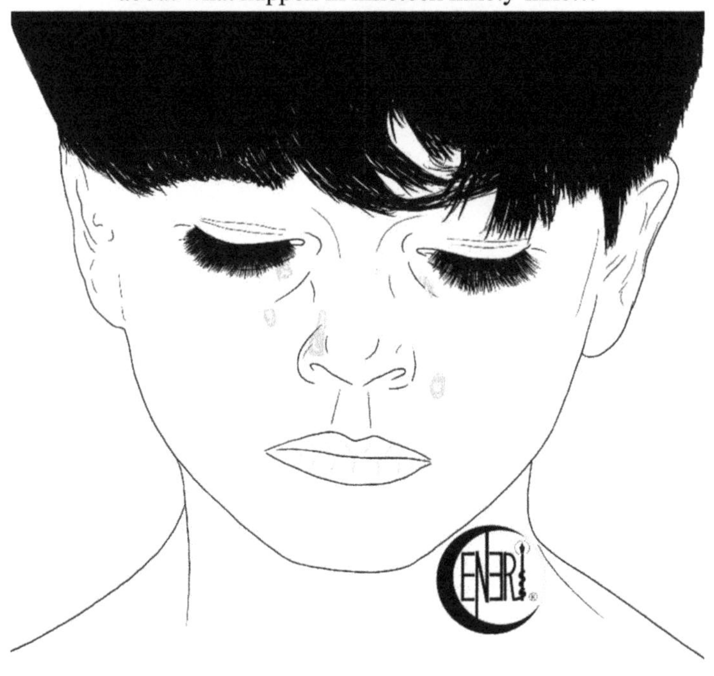

I'm a living dead
stiff and immobile I am here,
waiting for your return
while you are very happy without me.

At the time past I'm still looking for the reason!
Why and when I failed?
I just had the love in my hands, I let it go.
I though it wasn't for me, that's why I decided
not to look for you anymore…
If you're mine, you will comeback,
if you're not, nothing is going to happen anymore…

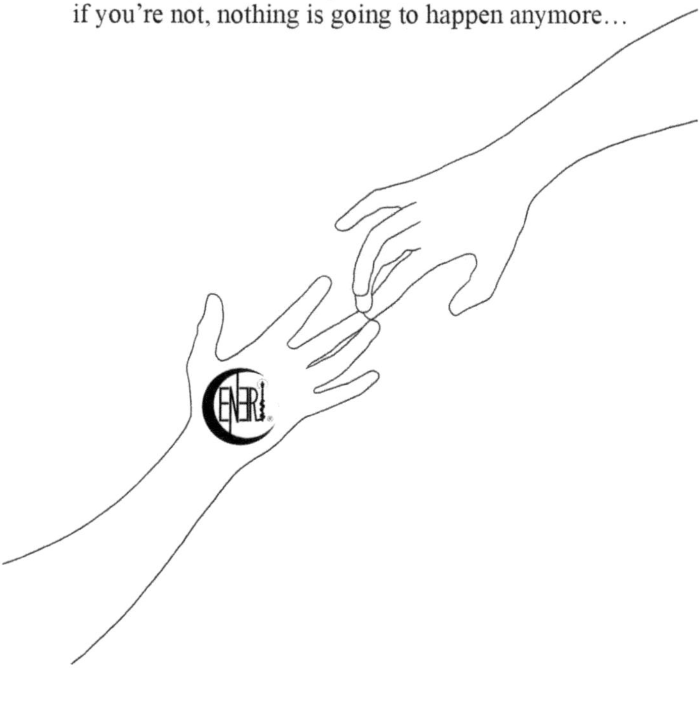

I still remember that loving being,
that due to problems I had to abandon him.
I will never forget him,
because although I am far from looking at him,
in my heart I must keep him
and I must also always remember him.

Some nights you see when I cry
but you never see when I try
to tell you what I feel inside,
maybe it's that you are too shy.
Perhaps you don't want to know the why
I still love you so much.
When all you do is give me dislikes
and all that makes me really sad.
But I still love you and for that
I now bury you in the depth of my heart.

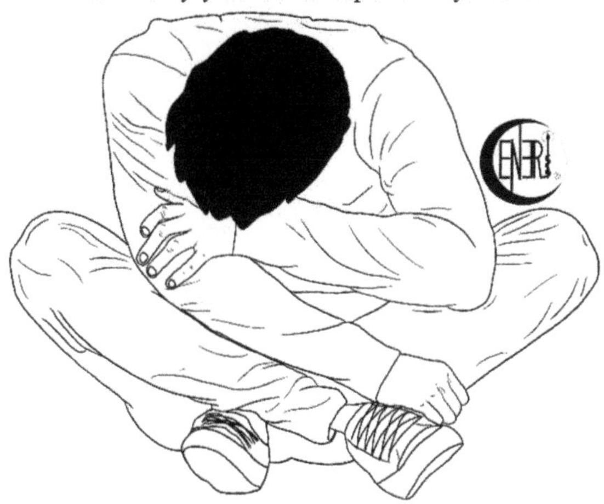

Loneliness weighs on my soul,
my heartbeat screams its pain
and among so many sounds of silence,
in a day like this my soul was lost.

Repenting our mistakes is useless,
because the past doesn't give do overs,
and even if the past could be changed,
I wouldn't trade the lessons
those mistakes teach us.

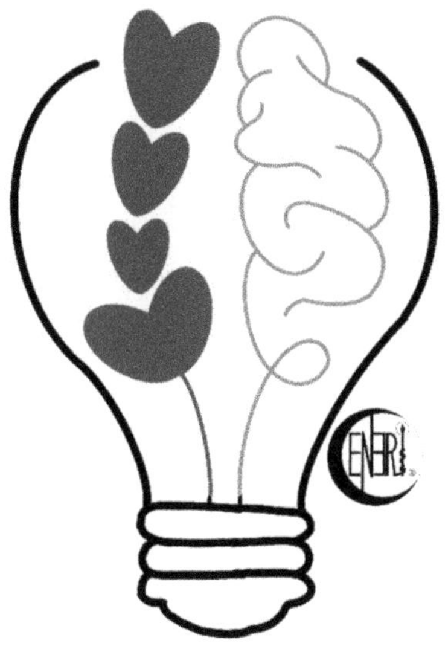

Your personality is so rude
and it kills my illusion,
it that takes away my joy
and it breaks my heart.

The nights that I've lived
they are very long to tell,
complaining and crying for my cold loneliness,
that kills me like the cold of the Titanic undersea.

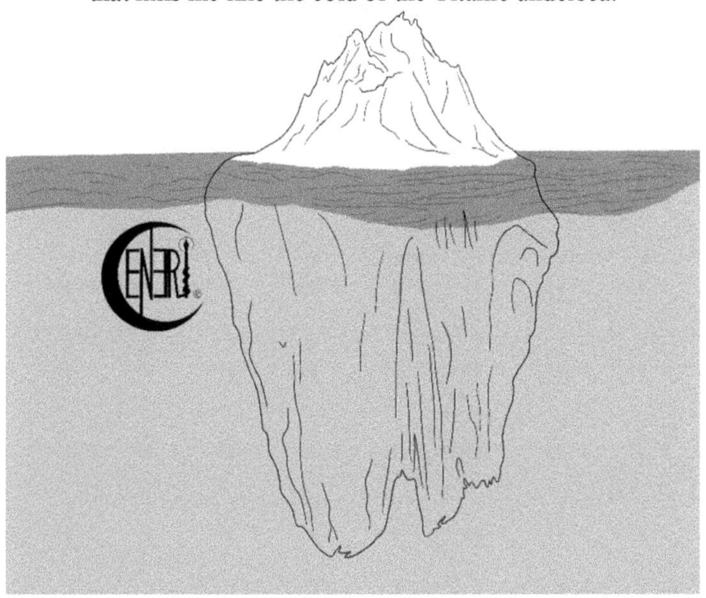

Castles and maidens
they are stories and tales,
that appear on TV for little girls
to learn that they need a man to save them.

God knows my thoughts,
my present and my past,
how I cried and how I scream,
without being able to shoot myself.

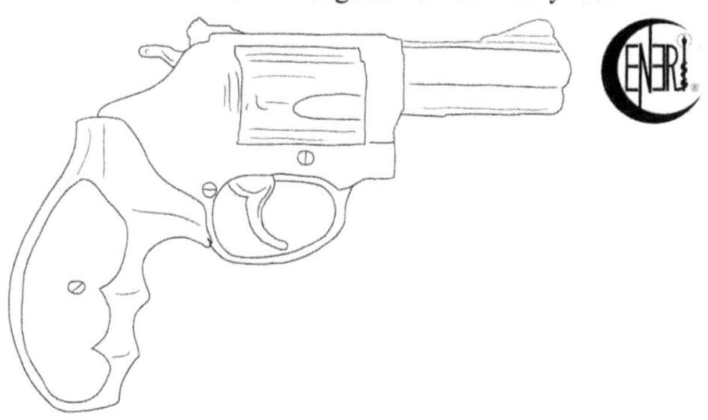

122

I feel like life is leaving me in seconds
and I cannot do anything,
to get this stake out of me
that you left in me nailed.

Our kisses and caresses
they are just a game,
that appear out of nowhere
because love is an unfair game.

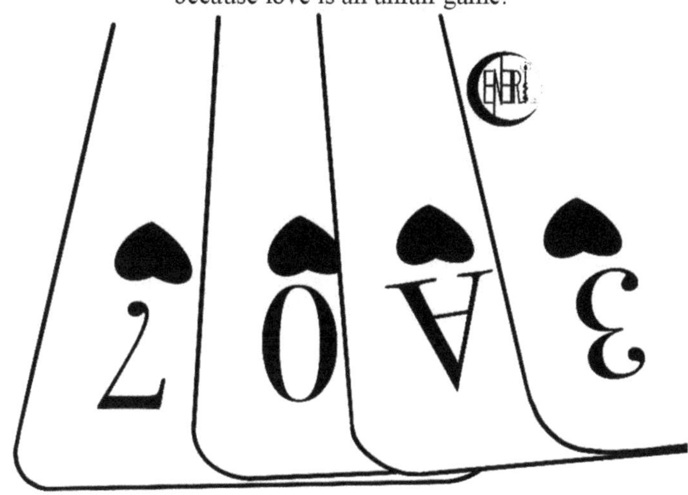

I feel miserable
because nothing goes right.
I feel the world falling over me
and I can't even move.

Tender, simple and beautiful... the love you gave me,
without thinking that your love was just empty words,
that your damn crafty mind happily invented them,
to rip my heart off and I foolishly like an idiot adored you.

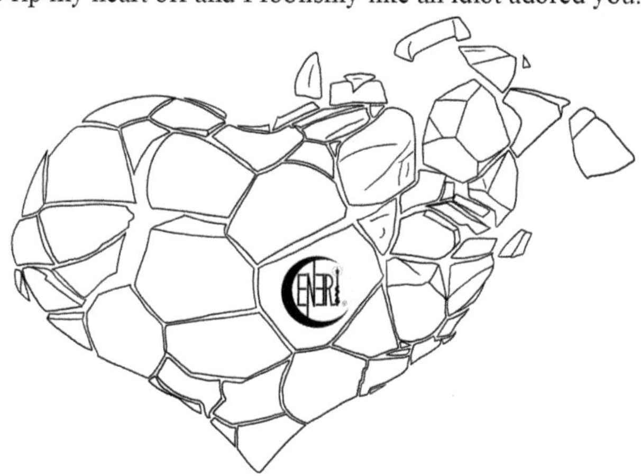

Crying is useless
when the pain is so deep
nothing comforts you
until you see the end of the world.

From loneliness I come
and to solitude I go,
thinking about the heartaches
that our hearts collect.

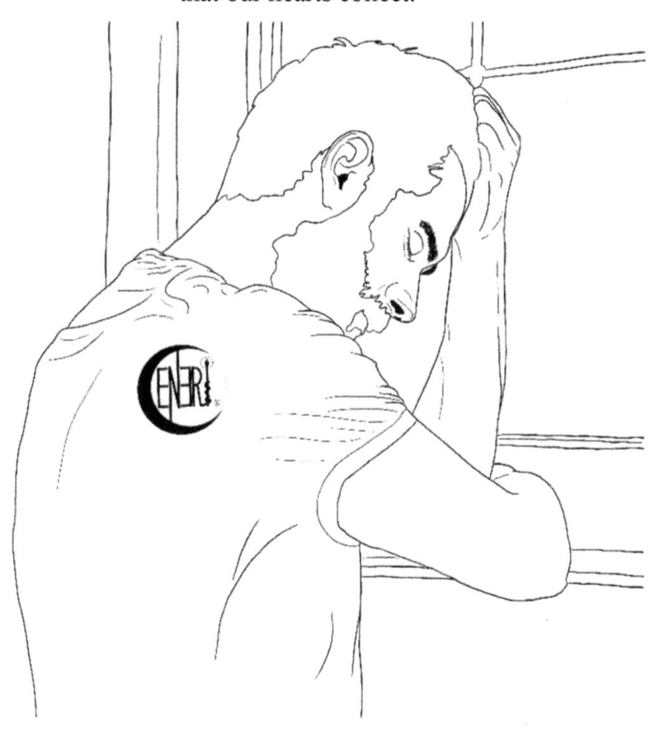

Adric Ceneri

I think you love me
while you cheat on me,
with your stuff and bullshit
that with pleasure and laughter you plot.

The person I love hurt my heart
and left me like a dog crying for his love,
I was to blame for confessing my love
and so now I suffer mercilessly with my pain.

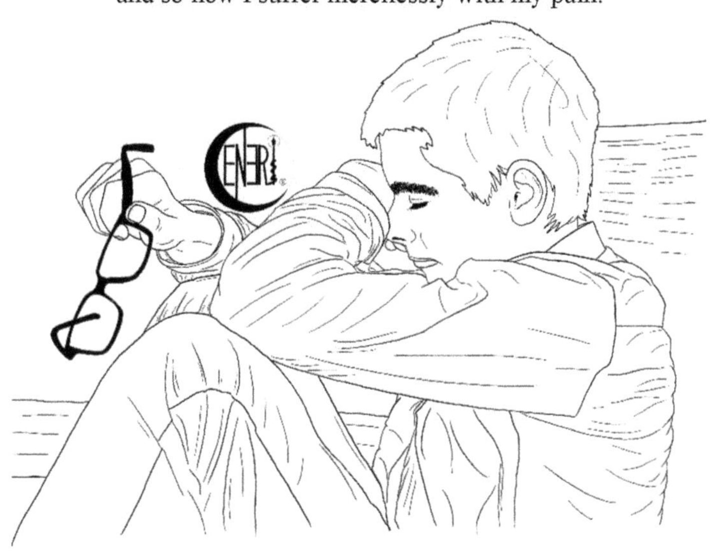

The sadness of my heart
can't stand the pressure
of my agony and depression anymore
that I face every day without illusions.

How difficult it is to live
with something that makes you suffer,
and how difficult it is to continue
with the hurtful wounds in you.

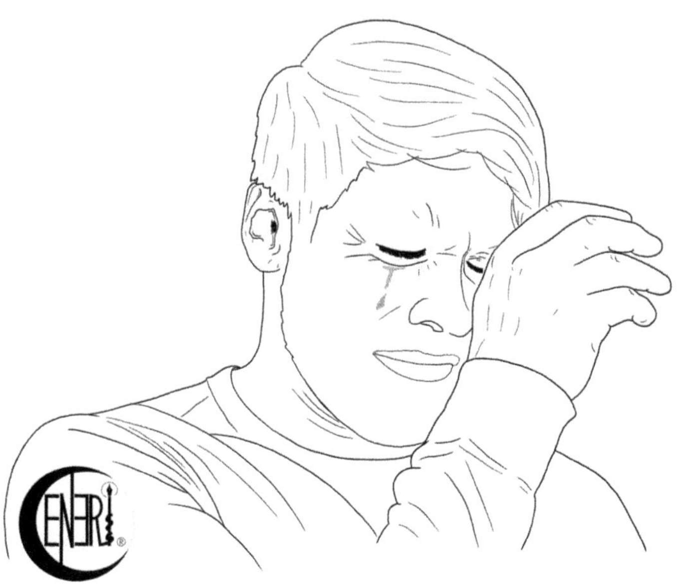

How I wish I hadn't met you, but I already did,
you don't know how much I regret
to have met you at that point in time,
if I had known who you were,
today I wouldn't be in this hell...

Days go by and I can't do anything
to stop time that goes by like nothing
and this pity in my soul that tortures me daily,
it mutilates me and I can't find peace.

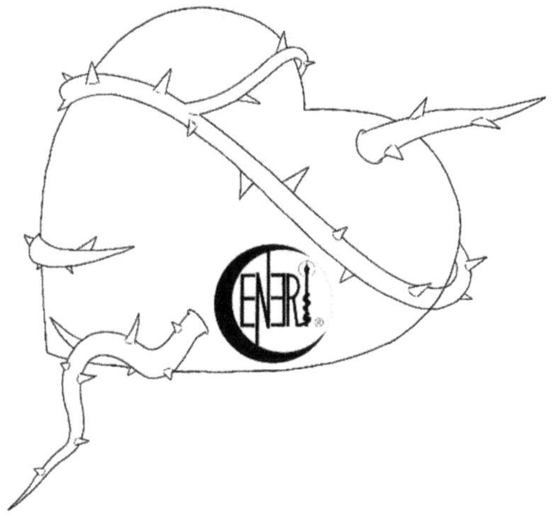

What happened to me? I was a boy.
Why don't you forget me? I'm not your toy.
You need to believe me, I'm your son.
Please don't ignore me. I'm a person.

Today I'm right here, tomorrow I don't know where,
maybe right there or perhaps in hell,
but I do not know or understand,
where to go or where to stay?

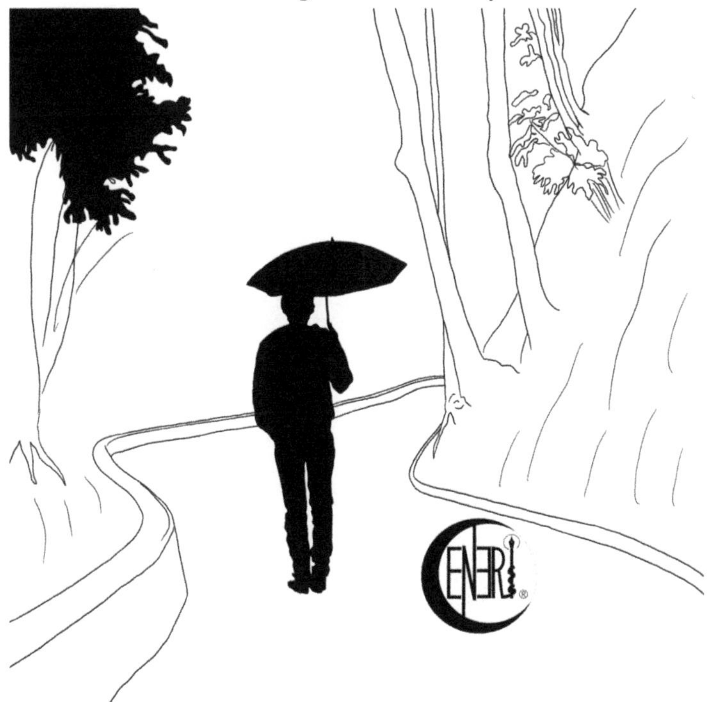

And just when I thought
we could have our happy ending.
They took you away from me,
and I was not able to do anything.
Nothing is right and this is madness,
I am scared and I feel helpless.

My soul dried up due to all the time I wasted waiting,
for a love that never came and today,
I am only sad, lonely and bitter...
Despite of still being in love with you.

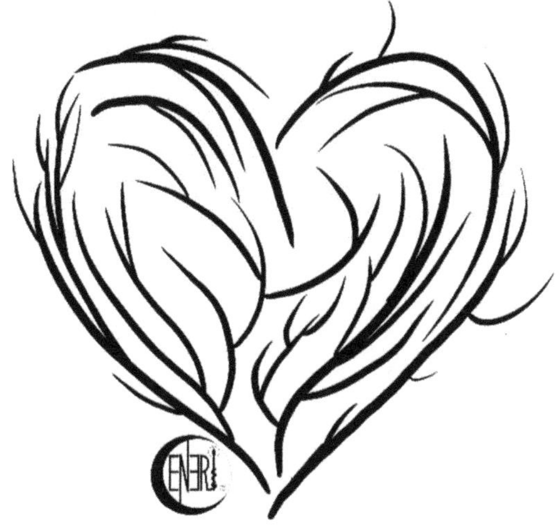

I once dreamed of a blue sky with veil clouds,
a gray river, opaque with sadness.
Carrying the blood of its highness.
The furious wind screams in it sings,
the night returns and covers the day with its cloak.

My heart is hurt and nobody can understand me,
because no one has felt what it feels like to lose themselves
in a deep abyss, in which death reigns
and I was so close to die on her chains.

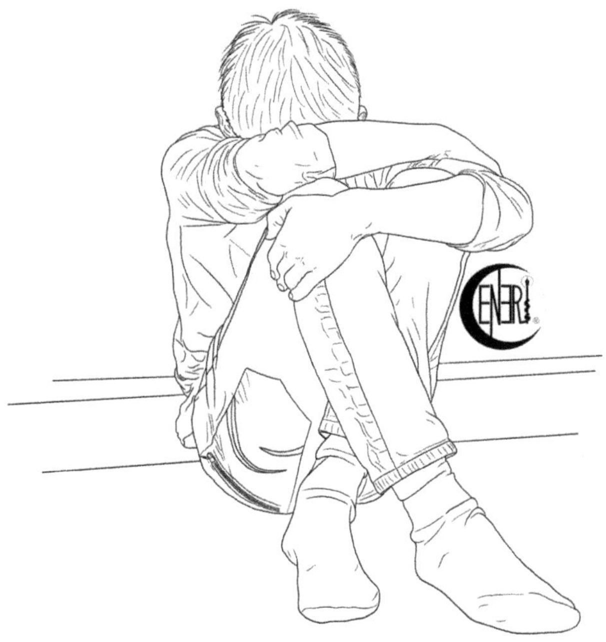

The wound I have is very difficult to heal
and throughout every thought
I still haven't managed to find,
the correct answer to this reality
that I live over and over but I can't ever wake up.

Only one wing to fly, only one tear to cry,
only an opportunity to try,
only one person to be mine,
or could be death who might make me die

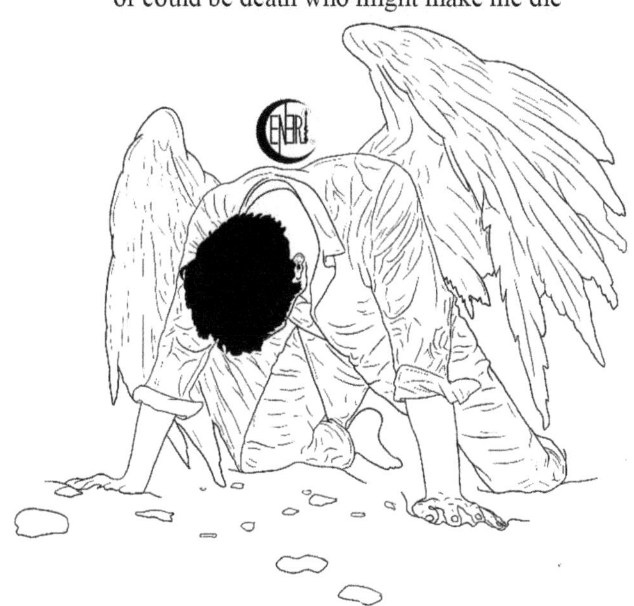

Why do we have to look for friends?
Where we know they're not,
we better let them come in
that one day… they should be here.

REFLECTIONS
Short Stories

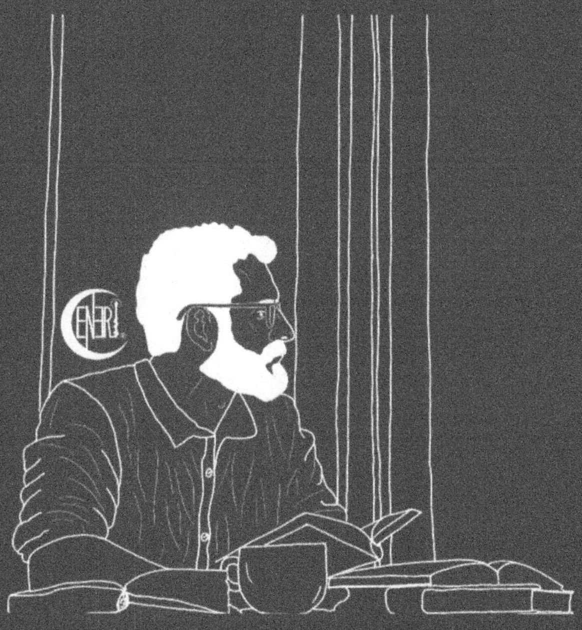

AFRAID TO BE LOST

Just a few years ago, I flew away from my house,
looking for shelter where I could stay at.
Destiny and time aren't the same – no they're not!
Years have passed and everything looks alike.
One less pair of roses but one pair of sorrows added.

Just a few centuries ago, loneliness was among us,
I ran away, leaving my past behind.
Life changed but my memories bothered my mind,
it was my garden and children, our house,
an abyss in agony
and these sorrows are giving me a hard time.

Just a few months ago, my daughter went on her own,
looking for a road full of freedom.
Time has passed and I see that she is falling apart.
The wedding was beautiful but the divorce will end it all.
Life isn't easy, but we have motives to fight.

Just a few days ago, my son said he is leaving,
looking for his dreams and his life's hopes.
It's his decision and I will miss him very much/
There're just a few days left before he walks away,
it's the blood in my veins, the power to overcome.

I'm afraid to stay alone,
but soon or later, I'll be lost.
My heart screams,
it asks, how much time will we have to leave
before the sky falls apart,
before the desert and the sea fuse as one?

ANONYMOUS LETTER

I don't know how to let you know.
How can I tell you what I feel?
I need you close before this love gets lost.
I want you with me, everywhere I go.
I want you to dedicate me a song sometime.

Baby, I love you, of it you can be sure…
I wouldn't like to lose you.

I wish you could call me sometime,
so, I can feel that you are interested in me.

For sure, I am not a stone,
I have feelings as any human being in this world.

You're right… I do have a busy life,
but that doesn't mean we will never have time for us.
We just need to work it out, to get rid of this chaos.

I hope you understand and comprehend me,
open your eyes and see who I am.
Excuses in this world are just a waste of time,
I will not buy your colorful lies.

I understand we need our own space,
but the problem is you always want your single space.

I love you and deep inside I wish you understood,
and hopefully you wake up before it's too late.

I wish you could stop me from leaving you alone.
I don't wish to walk away because this couldn't work.

THE CHOOSING

There's freedom in this world, and having freedom is power.
If you have it, you can solve all obstacles like it's nothing.

There're many things in this world,
things that we must to live to be certain of.
There're many ways to live, and having one is good for all.

Because that describes our dreams,
and the person we can be.
There are many kinds of souls looking to live
like the one who's writing this.

Get to know me now folks, that I'll have to leave soon.
I've been dreaming too much,
please don't come and waste my time.

I've been losing lots of time,
I don't want to lose more than that.

There're many kinds of love, and having one is happiness.
If you have it, you'd know, that it's better than being alone.

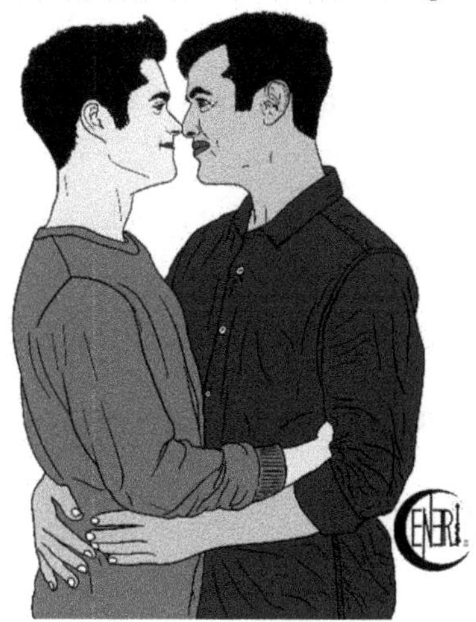

LIFE

For good or bad, life always turns against us,
as something without importance, feelings without trust.

Until now, nobody knows how we arrived here.
Scientists say that we came from evolution,
others say we come from God according to their religion.

What I know is that I don't have the solution,
this has been a controversy
that won't end in my version.

Life was beautiful; today, it isn't more than a lost illusion.

Once I thought to fall in love with the right person,
but love arrived without requesting my authorization.

Life and death have two things in common,
both are unexpected and feelings just go on.
Feelings never warn, they just come to make their work,
good or bad, nevertheless, our worth concerns them.

If you can't win against your memories,
unite your strength and destroy your soul.
Don't let weakness take you away from this world.

Hypocrisy is not good;
although who cares what I am here for.
I'm just an individual who is not a saint of devotion.

The planet is big, but I am able to make it shrink.
The dreams are illusions,
just as the creations of my mind.

The Winter approaches,
while a year announces its goodbye.
Life is a waste of space where I can't breathe at all.
Rivers, lakes and seas show me the end of this life.

They show me the end of this planet,
a world full of sins and lies,
a land of problems,
agonies and diseases that soon will fall apart.

Life was beautiful, but today is no longer the same.
Time ago I was a boy, a boy who I won't ever be again.
The cold Winter moves away,
then Summer return with its hot rays.

Yesterday, I was somebody; today,
I'm not more than a shade.
Yesterday, the meadows used to be green and alive,
but today they're dead and dry.
Time ago I was a kid; today,
I'm no more than a lost guy.

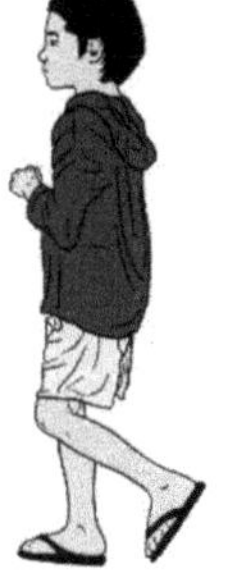

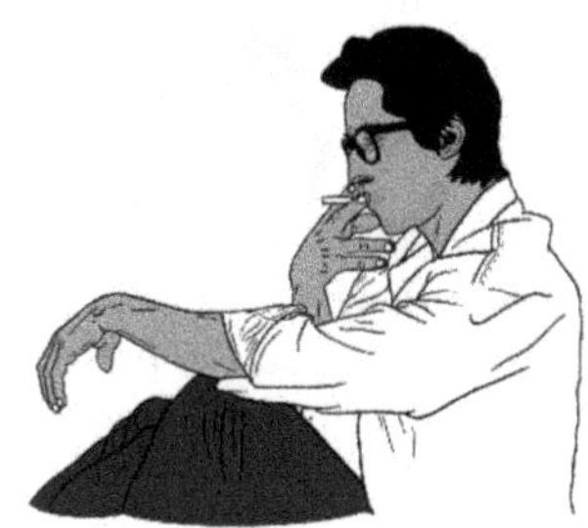

MIND PUZZLE

Out here, everything is confusion.
In occasions, it's hard to figure out…
the truth and secrets are hidden under deep lies.

Black and white… colors in life left.
As afraid of losing everything you are,
as if bad things never happen – when it's going to stop?
An example; antonyms… the opposite side of things.

The roads and coincidences for people are sensational,
so what do I care if that's right.

Humans base their lives upon lies.
Everything to be the perfect story,
trash words that confuse their minds.

Fake stories created by humans,
allusions that are never wise,
as tomorrow, everything could fall.
I control my life.
I won't let anyone tell me crap.
I like no one controlling my mind.

I love freedom and I love my heart.
I think everybody should be who they are.
There is no reason to pretend.
No reason to be who you're not.

Just because it's the best way to show who we are.
Let life go as if everything was right.

These are just mind puzzles,
lost, manipulated thoughts in our minds,
it's done… goodbye.

THE BABY'S DREAMS

To be the first one, the winner of all of us.
I run as fast as possible till I get to where I am.
I'm growing slowly inside of you,
but sometimes I feel like jumping a lot.
I do know… you don't sleep well at night,
and during the day you have a job.

You're tired, before the evening starts.
Oh, poor mother of mine, all this you do for my life.
I can feel your caresses over your skin,
your warm and soft hands sleep me during the day.

I want you to take me in your arms.
I wish to know how much you're prepared to give for your son.
No matter what happens, I want you to know,
I will always love you mother, and you can have my love.
I thank you for letting me grow in your belly.
Thank you for loving and waiting for me
with your heart and arms open.

I know I still don't have reasoning,
but soon I'll be able to be.
Please always love me, and I will do the same…

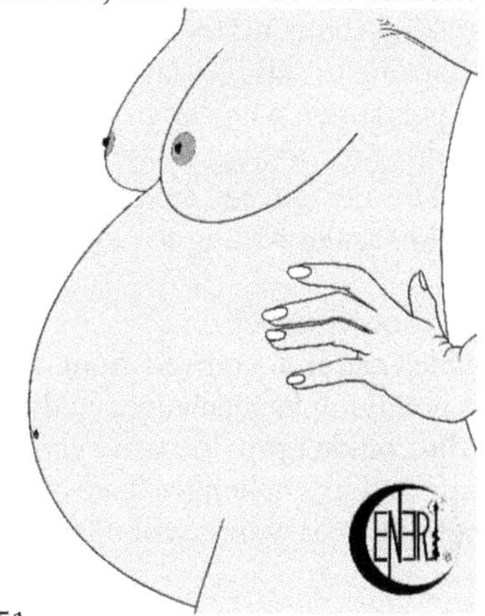

151

THE ESCORT

Ariana, the women seduced by large amounts of money,
every night she let in clients between her legs.

An elegant prostitute,
who has perfect breasts and flawless curves.
Dangerous… but beautiful,
capable of making any men's dreams come true.

Ironic… yes!
But what's truly ironic
is that she knows it's erotic.

She must pretend to love and lust,
she can't ever sell her heart.

It's sad to choose rich and wealthy men
who can offer and provide anything you want.
What's even sadder…
is knowing her heart belongs to another guy.

She's the perfect escort, wearing her flirtatious red dress
and her high heels every night,
modeling her legs sensually,
making some money and losing the love of her life,
choosing to sell pleasure and sex,
to gentlemen who can pay very well.
In this life, nothing is simply free,
and beauty and sex are part of the top sales
to those men willing to pay.

To choose money…
which can free yourself from poverty, at last,
is not dying in shame, nor in the arms of a man
who couldn't provide what you needed from him.
Life and its challenges have consequences...
nothing is easy, nor will it ever be.

An inner solitude,
cold and depressive can present itself, but this is a circus,
which has a price that has to be paid.

Maybe it's not worth it.
Who really could prove it?
Who in the blessed heaven
or in the damned hell could possibly clarify?
How tragic and so difficult would life be,
between sex, drugs, and alcohol?
Why is it that life is relentless
with us and our pain?

Her death couldn't even be perfect,
Oh, beautiful princess, queen and goddess of hookers with heels!
Luxurious the decades when you danced
in the bar of Don Simón,
today you are just another story... an essence of pain.

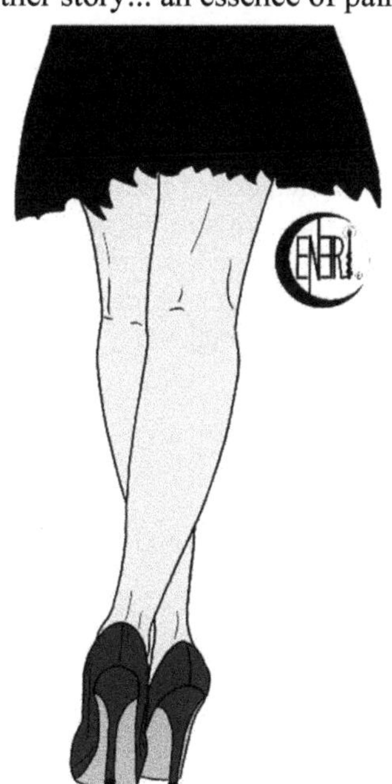

THE ARTIST

The brush and the paint...
they can create great figures,
Of course, they could never paint
your greatest fear or your illogical follies.

The fame that elevated your ego...
Couldn't raise your dreams
but it did throw them away in the trash,
it sold your love and your madness,
it's simply disappointing to see a life collapse.

I see eyes that no longer shine,
between hands that painted are now cold,
while the painted flowers wither,
a train called destiny comes to pick up your pale soul.

The inks and colors...
sometimes they can be very optimistic,
it's obvious that never enough for an artist.

Those illusions of being beyond mere sight,
today they are nothing more
than a myth among magazines,
sounds without a voice,
lies without laughter.

That artist with sturdy and battered hands,
with honey eyes,
that one day brightened with hope,
he ended up losing this battle,
ended up losing hair, skin,
and then he lost the desire,
his forces to fight against cancer that killed him,
for fear and pain to see how his body,
suffer from chemotherapy.

Sad to see that despite everything
we aren't as strong,
sad... even more so
when we give up admitting defeat,
the failure of an artist
was not to have faith,
it was not to be brave,
the thread broke and with it his present.

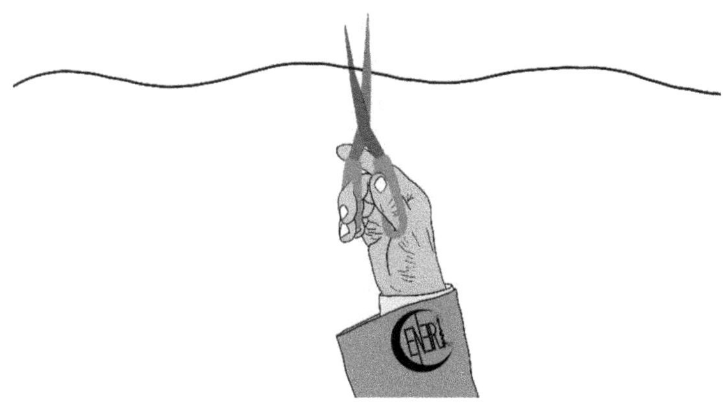

THE PRICE TO CHANGE

It hurts to see that what we believe it's more lie than truth,
it hurts even more when we trust,
when they put a dagger in our backs.

Journalists write articles
that people without occupation have to criticize.

Photographers capture moments,
special memories that not everyone could catch.

The writers write arguments,
between rhymes and lines its darkest reality.

Each profession has a price,
a high cost that must be paid,
it's difficult to accept it,
but it's the work that each one chooses to carry out.

The singers today sing only to sing,
they no longer do it with that joy, not as they sang before!

The actors behind a disguise
in every scene and work of art,
they always look for a way not to fail.

The song writers have been running out,
there is no many song writers out there
and every day there are more artists who want to sing.

If this is what we call life,
who could change that?
Who could be brave enough,
to transform this present
and reset the clock of lies?

OLD SOULS

As I wake up one dark morning of February.
I see another day… I feel lonely on my own way.
I have memories, nothing else left.

I have stories, history from our parents.
It was past times.
There're ashes left, now there are no fights.

These are the wonders; these are our moments.
This is your story, pieces of a complement.
There is no reason not to do what I feel.
The root of life crashed into my fears.

My life is overcoming, yours is gone.
It hurts now, and in few days, it's done.

Without your permission, it took you away.
It will also take me one of these days.

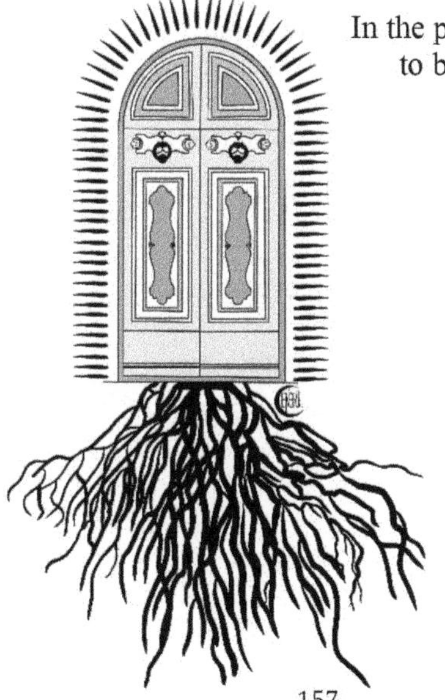

In the paradise, I will see you,
to be once again with you.

CONFESSION OF THE PAST

I just wanted to see my wish come true,
I wanted to make my heart feel one more time.

I no longer am, but yesterday I was.
When he died, I was born.
It's difficult to feel calm when there's a cross on your back.
It's not difficult to lose your soul
when the reason is no longer here.

I was someone but now I'm heading towards the light.
Dying is not as bad,
not as terrible and empty as being a reflection.

The veil of night falls on the wind,
and it spreads its coldness, the stars shine, but not as before.
What yesterday was, today isn't, nor will tomorrow be.
Just as I was born yesterday, today I die
and tomorrow my grave will not remain.

My life was so short, as you can't imagine,
I lived, felt and enjoyed abusively, as long as I could,
today I leave with my soul full, but my body tore.
I died in a sunset... when shots were fired from a gun,
the wounds that those pieces of iron
made me were so lukewarm.

Every shot, every wound stole a piece of my life,
until my eyesight vanished.
I think it was a dream, not a nightmare,
that's how I died in another life.

MARKINGS

Poetry and art are my reality,
are the letters and the lines,
it's the history kept for eternity.

It's very true, nothing lasts forever,
but history proves prudent.

Show the yesterday and the present,
shows loneliness and shows forgetfulness,
they're the drops of rain,
the tears of very sensitive eyes.

Life takes us to different paths,
makes and undoes our destinies,
yesterday I ran from the blows and abuses,
today with my head held high I'm a desire.

I live and do with my life what I want.
I'm a human, someone proud
of who he is, not what he is.
I go with the wind and I sleep with the sunset,
I wake up and I live in each sunrise.

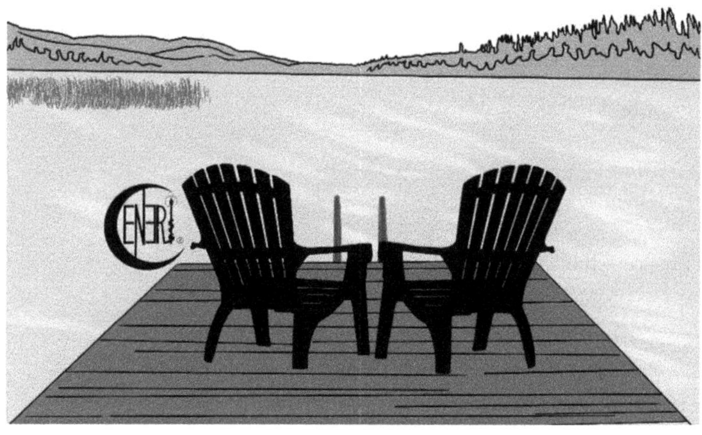

PRETENSE

Sometimes things
They're not what they appear to be,
we cover the truth under false disguises,
cheating ourselves,
for not wanting to see the truth.

The reality of life can be more than cruel,
a dark dawn,
we walk towards the perfect world created by a belief,
and we hide the errors, as if nothing happened.

Today I'm afraid of wounds, to be hurt again.
I'm afraid that my heart will break again.

The mirror screams at me...
it tells me how pathetic I am,
but I don't believe him, and I shut myself in fear.

Today I want to think, impossible...
yesterday my mind vanished,
it vanished with the air,
with the night, as well as when the sun goes down.
If I could get rid of my feelings, I would,
to not feel more pain,
and if I could throw away my conscience,
I wouldn't doubt it,
to not feel this fault of my mistake.

We all have a dark being,
very deep within us,
and the roads that we chose
They're what distinguish who we are...

SEX AND LOVE

Making love is one thing,
having sex is another.

Making love comes from something lasting,
Having sex comes from something transient.

Loving is not just saying I love you.
Sex is just passion and fever ... nothing sincere.

These things are very similar,
but very different at the same time.

In both situations, the same thing happens,
but in sex, love of the good can't be.

This dilemma is just thinking about it,
and analyze it very well.

So, think about it, my friends,
It's something very serious about what we can learn.

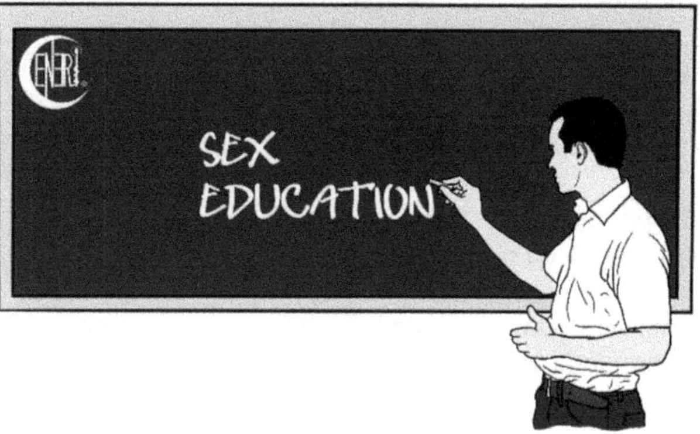

ADULTERY

The silence of your voice is mysterious,
words, letters, and verses.
The question is; Why adultery?
strong word, an atrocious sin.

Critics of a life,
one lover dead and another alive.

Soulmates... not the perfect couple.

Making mistakes has a prize,
with it, there's always the aftermath.

Deceptions under sinister eyes,
deep and dry gazes will rise.

For him, today you do everything,
tomorrow... for you he won't do anything.

You like him, yes...
you love him, I almost forgot.

Just as today you enjoy your desire and lust,
tomorrow with someone else he'll do
what you did yesterday with him in your bed.

The one who does it once,
will always do it again and again.

However, today you both kill each other's modesty,
making love without having words to be said.

As the two of you agreed to put out this heat,
to let it be and let it end on each other's flesh.

LOST SHEEP

The love of God... is greater than the universe,
it's his tests, his teachings, and his promises,
a sinner... that's me and the whole universe.
I'm no more than a lost sheep, far from heaven,
thinking of doing something and truly doing it isn't the same,
it's not the same to plan than to think about what could happen.
I admit that I'm doing wrong,
that in my dusk I may lose myself,
I could lose everything if I ever try to return.
Life's intent has always been to continue,
I reflect when thinking about reality,
When I see the stars, I find so many desires,
illusions that didn't become true,
I get nostalgic but I can't cry,
comets watch me ... criticize my pain.
God knows me, he who is great and always will be,
I already walked the beginning, and my sins I have accepted,
my life is not the wonder of the century,
but the gift of writing as I write,
it could only be the work of Jehovah.
In the end, it's always good to change,
feel the changes and believe that it never hurts.
Thanks for everything!... I hope not to fail.

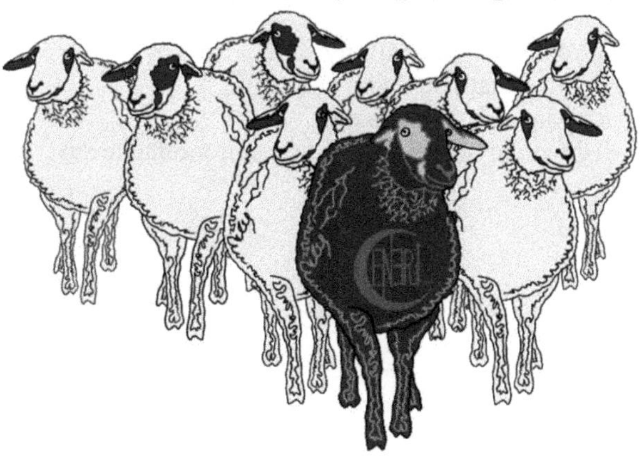

GIRL TO A WOMEN

Fifteen years have passed in the life of a girl,
who today has become a young lady.

That playful girl has started to become a woman,
the apple of my eyes who just yesterday was a baby.

It's a blessing that you're my daughter,
and today I want to please you,
today that you turn fifteen,
I want to see you happy and content
when you split your cake.

And at the time of your dance,
everything goes super well,
and you enjoy this party,
party that is only lived once.

That you share with us,
with everyone present,
even with those who aren't here,
and smile at the world,
no matter what happens
my girl you will never stop being.

You're the adoration of my soul,
something that you know very well,
that's why today on this day,
I wish you to have an amazing... unforgettable day.

THE SECRET

It seems like yesterday... when he was just a boy
when I thankfully stayed quiet to be alive today.

Where would I be? If I had not remained silent,
if I had not grieved alone, maybe I would've been killed.
Today I'm still here, and I need to confess my sins,
to tell my story, sorrows that my heart has saved.

A coincidence that happened, no more than twenty years ago,
I was abused, I was raped,
something repulsive that left me damaged.

It condemned my conscience, and it repressed my existence.
I was used for pleasure by force, at the cost of my tears, my pain...

Why? I don't know! And I probably will never know,
What reason is there for making a human being suffer?
What is the point of turning the life of a child into hell?

The time has passed, and I have overcome that great fear,
thoughts that sometimes made me feel confused.
Today my sorrows have been clarified...
My suicidal thoughts have vanished from my mind,
and I hope in God's justice
for all rape victims who have never speak up.

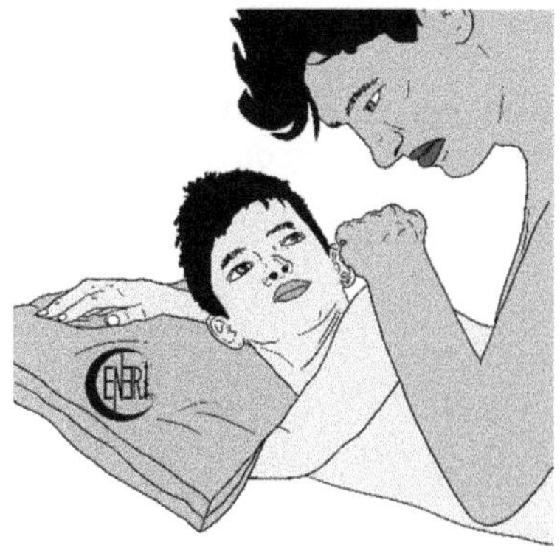

A CHALLENGE

I don't think it's my fault of what my feelings want,
I swear it wasn't my mistake,
it wasn't me who decided to be so uncertain.

Fate chose me to be different
so that I lived my life in a labyrinth.

The final challenge will be not to die...
To move forward without looking or hearing,
without hearing the insults,
without looking at the ignorance of people
who chose not to understand.

Nature is strange, so strange that there are still people,
ignorant people with backward mentalities.

I don't understand what is happening,
I don't understand what they feel!
How is it that they love?
Why can't this fucking society distill anything else
other than lectures and tragedies?

Why in the name of heaven
they don't use the faith they say they have
to begin trusting rather than continue judging as they do?...
so, we could live as humans, like civilized people, instead.

Today I swear before this writing,
that I will live without fear of any challenges,
to show everyone I succeeded... Because I did!

BEFORE

On some occasions, I came to think
that we would be together for the rest of eternity.

But realism taught me...
that it's difficult to obtain what one wants,
details that are sometimes small,
and for reasons unknown we never understand it.

Today, together, we are taking advantage of our moment,
let's do it for that tomorrow,
for that day where we will go our separate ways.

It's inevitable and it hurts me to think, the idea terrifies me,
I don't want to imagine that you'll forget me.

I don't know the truth and I'm curious to know,
I know it's easier to let you go than to see you pass away.
Maybe we're just a couple of good friends,
friends who have different lives and destinies.
Before you leave, make sure the door is closed,
so that our friendship is preserved to continue it in the future,
to prove to us that friendship exists and is carried in the soul.

That despite the time passed, this friendship is still fresh,
as in that day of our first open conversation.

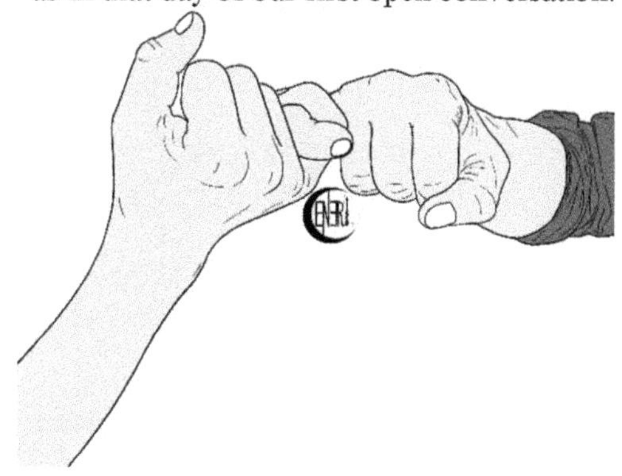

WAITING

Here I am on this day,
just sitting out here and thinking.

Remembering what my life was like,
and how I ended up in this village.

As I see the end approaching,
I feel that as days pass, I know more than yesterday,
I no longer believe in the wishes of comets.

I wait for the day to leave,
to go away,
if possible, to the farthest country.

The desire to be able to live,
far from so much falseness,
to live somewhere,
where it doesn't provoke me what I feel being here.

There are motives and there are reasons,
that no one can never understand,
desires of fear...
crazy and feigned thoughts.
Little by little,
time annihilates these feelings,
turns our dreams into stone,
and turns our fears to ash.

NEVER-ENDING JOURNEY

The purity of your soul...
It's transparent and crystal clear,
where I find calm when there is no other way out
of my daily problems, the ones I face every day,
trying to dodge them
without thinking about the wounds,
that over the years have stayed in my life.

Also, those failures that torment me day after day,
but I'll continue... and I'll fight
until the strength runs out
until my feet no longer resist
neither the pain nor the breakdown,
that has made me cry for years.

Tears that fell from my face and evaporated in my soul,
now I will find calmness,
peace, tranquility and my longed-for happiness.
In the end,
we will both walk in the long and never-ending journey.

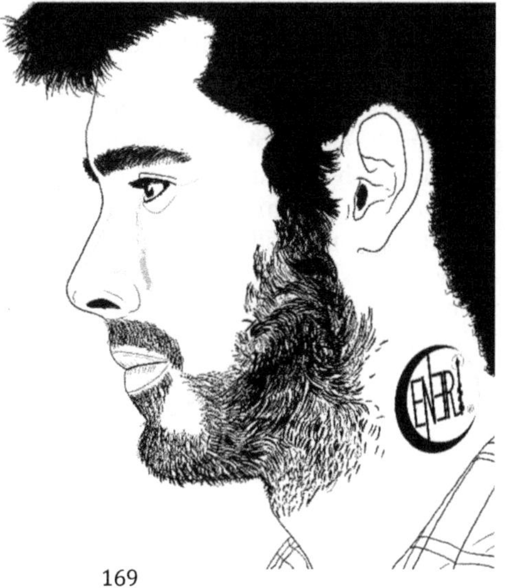

HATE CRIME

A morning like any other,
running towards the park crossing the road,
you arrive at your house and you find a surprise,
new neighbors and they are from the church,
they're homophobic but you don't realize,
you run into danger don't open the door,
take care of yourself... and your partner.

Beware the danger lurks, don't be distracted, stay alert,
it's too late, your beloved hasn't come back home,
you're going to look for him and luckily you find him
on the verge of death, but he clings to life.

It's the ambulance that takes him,
a crime without justice, a murder without conscience,
now you look for those who are guilty,
to pay for what they've done,
but you still don't know, who is to blame for this pain.

Everyone knows that the one who seeks finds,
and when searching, you find clues to your answers,
little by little, you are closer to the truth.

In the name of God, a murderer sin,
and he makes a mistake without thinking about the law,
you look for help, but the police don't care
about a crime committed, an act without decency.
You discover the truth and it isn't what you had imagined,
and as you try to expose those who are guilty,
the police ignore your case and disregards it,
failing you to providing the demanded justice.

So, you take justice in your own hands,
with the help of your mother-in-law, who suffers pain,
his son was hurt, and he was killed, taken from her as well.

An ambush, it's a great idea,
kill him and blame him for invading your home,
make people believe that you killed him in your defense,
to do justice above the government and its forces.

You have peace, but you still can't accept this fate,
you don't want to forget, in your heart your lover remains,
in your mind, there's still that memory that feeds
your desire to live, even if you don't have him close.
It was unexpected, but the past doesn't return,
you're still alive, don't let your guard down,
life and time keep passing and they don't return,
but your end is not this one and the stars shine on you.
You're still here today in the present day,
you're alone and your lover only exists in your mind,
there's nothing more, but to say how much it hurts,
to love... blindly, and feel that you still want him back.

On a train, he leaves, with a ticket without return,
the wind warns you, that he isn't here anymore,
and the moon sings for your sad loneliness,
the rain falls and you still remember him,
the time continues to pass and the Christmas snow arrives.

The visible magic vanished, and your love for him stayed,
everything went away and with it your pain,
but not your life... nor your love, that remained.

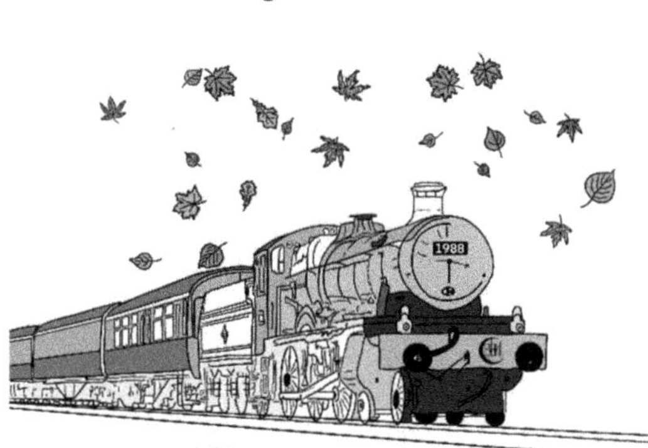

SUMMER

You have fears,
about discovering your identity.
You have fears and secrets
that you don't want to talk about.
You have doubts about yourself
and you fear the truth.

It's time for the party,
but you need no costume...
There are people like you,
don't be afraid of reality.

You are what you want to be,
not what they want you to be,
don't be afraid of your feelings.
Let yourself be loved!

The lake between mountains is a place without society,
although it's the nest of your secret when you want it to be,
next to someone you love secretly and in solitude.

You pretend to have a girlfriend,
and that you love her,
all for not wanting to admit who you are,
and refuse to change your lifestyle.

You're afraid of the unknown
and let your ideas fly.
It's summer, and you are in a camp,
the problems and conflicts face your truth.

There are three groups of people...
you don't know where your place is.
The boys who are different,
who enjoy their life.
Or the group of boys you grew up with,
in your hometown.
Or perhaps the one with beautiful girls,
but who you don't feel attracted to.

You're confused,
but in the end, everything will pass.
Just let time go by and your doubts will clear up.

There's no reason to hide in the woods
and start crying,
for someone who doesn't love you,
and who's happy with his girlfriend.
The summer is over,
a storm hits incessantly.
In the forest, lightning falls
and destroys a collapsing tree.

Time to go and return to your home with your family,
Allow time to pass, your doubts will be clarified.

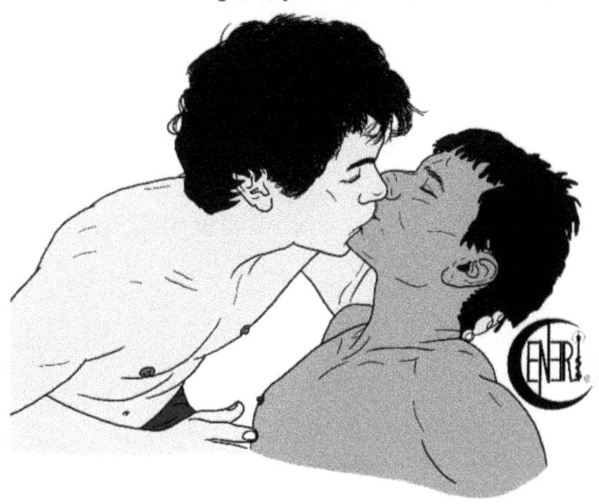

FORGIVE ME

Maybe I'm not the best of all poets,
but from the depths of my soul I give you two roses;
one for whenever you are feeling sad
and the other to tell you how beautiful you are.

I ask God to bless you,
may he always illuminate your path.
I know you're not my only friend
but in my life,
you hold a special place in my heart.

Friend, I don't know how to explain to you,
how to tell you that I'm sorry,
for wanting to help you in your love life,
I almost lost your friendship.

Accept my apologies and let's leave this behind,
I promise not to let you down, I won't do it again.
I hope our friendship can grow.
and that you and I remain friends,
for a few more decades.

CHAPTER 8

LOVE LETTERS
Love Stories

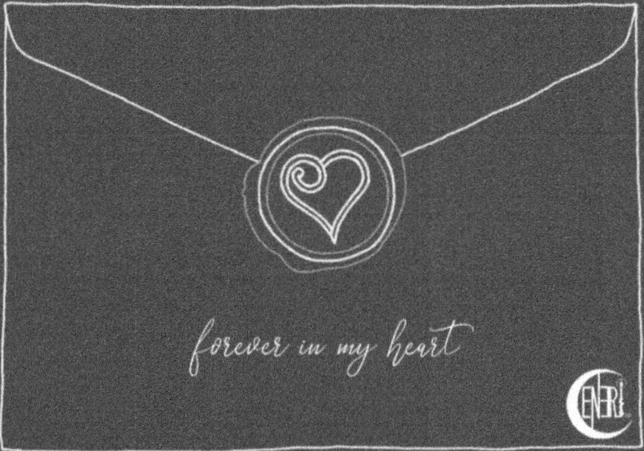

WISHES

I don't know who you are,
but I feel like I already love you!
My heart waits for you next to the stars,
So, its owner will be you.

I want you and for you…
I'm waiting impatiently and hopeless.
You are my illusion when I dream;
hopefully, with me you can be sincere.

Fortunately, you can love me,
with no intention of losing me,
because at the end, I don't want just a good bye,
I want to see you later and your memories in my mind.

I want to have true love for a long time,
love that can last in our lives.
I want someone who I can cry with,
dream, have fun, and laugh.

I want a person who can achieve his goals.
A person who can receive love;
a human who can share his world.

I want someone,
with whom I can walk next to
at the edge of the beach under the moonlight.

Look at the stars and talk about us,
to feel that someone loves me
and to keep it in my heart,
or put it into a crystal bottle for a long time.

THE WORLD WITH YOU

It's beautiful to travel around the world,
although having someone
would be better than being alone.
Doesn't matter
if the Lord's Angels will always be with me
to protect me,
to take care of me.

From the deepest of my heart,
I wish to have someone with me.

I wish for someone
who could show me love.
I wish to have someone to walk with,
to where I go,
just a person,
just a boy.

The shadows of the dark night
covered my path,
and with it,
painful memories come back.
I'm driving without direction,
without a destination.
It's beautiful to travel around the world,
although knowing I love someone
makes me feel less lost.
Doesn't matter
if death will always be after me,
because God will always defend me.

I don't wish
more than having you in my life.
I want nothing
but to have you with me in this world.
I want to have you
for at least a few minutes,
I want you and I want to be loved.

The sunrise comes out
and shows me my future,
and with it,
the best love in the universe.
I'm driving and you're with me
going to infinity.

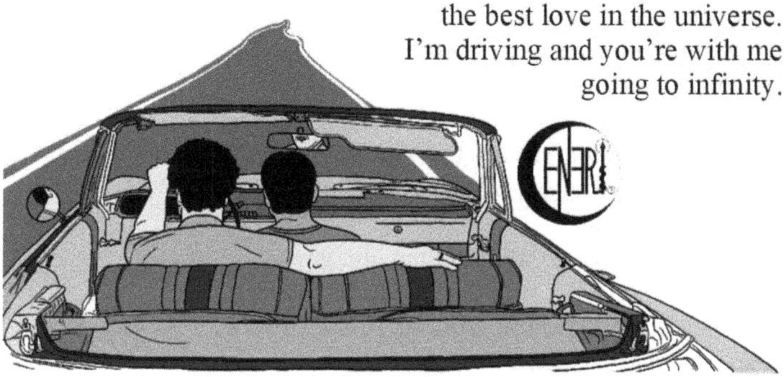

LOVE DECLARATION

The distance between us
isn't longer than my love.
I'm yours in all the ways you can think of.
I'll be yours forever,
you'll be mine twenty-four, seven.
There are no more engagements —
nothing can stop me, baby!

For you I'll do,
make and even cross the whole universe.
It doesn't matter when or how,
but that you be there waiting.
I need you honey; I need you ready;
I need you now, before it's too late.
Don't ever leave, if so, come back later.

I'm what you see; no more than a crazy.
Someone who offers true love without wonder.
Don't leave me here, not without you in my life.
Every morning, as I wake up,
you are the one I have on my mind.

You are the hope, the illusion, happiness and luck.
During the night full of stars,
we're looking at each other's sight.
I want you to know what I feel inside.
I prefer you to stay here, in my arms.

Stay with me, at least for this last night.
Let's make of our love;
the worst and best of our lives.
I need you beside me, here close to my heart.

You're the dream of my dreams, the pupil of my eyes.
You're the reason my heart never lies.
I don't need more reasons to love you.
I don't need an excuse to decide that I'll be waiting for you.

I'm fine just knowing I love you.
The trust between us is strong as a stone.
The sky is gray and cries,
Although your arms for me are always open wide.

Time fades away and leaves his mark.
The night is cold,
but your arms are soft and warm.

I love you for all we have.
I'll say it without shame or any remorse.
I'll say it here, in a sheet of paper,
paper which might get lost.
But my love's bright and will not fade if I have your soul.

Stay here, close to me at any cost.
I offer you love, love that doesn't have a price.
Love that is yours, but that option is not mine...

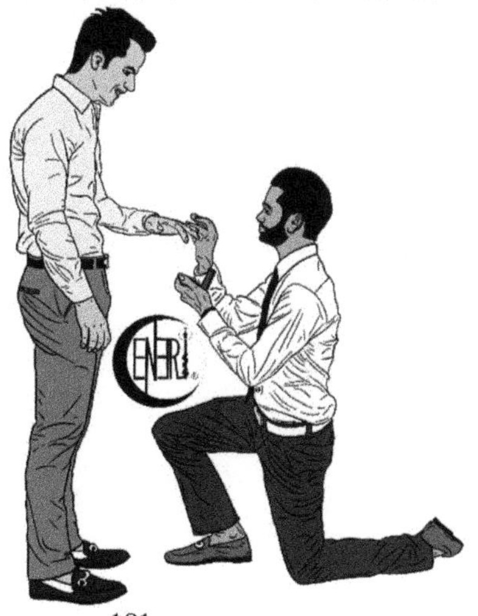

POEM TO MY MOTHER

On this Mother's Day,
I just want to tell you one thing.
This poem is for you, mother,
and I want you to take this joyfully.

So that you always remember me,
as an amazing person.

When I look at this poem,
I want you to feel proud.

Proud to be the best of mothers,
a great person, and lady.

You have a son who loves you,
and even if he does not show it,
he loves you above all,
in the same way that anyone can love
a fighting and warrior mother.

Maybe I'm not the best child, nor the best person,
even so... I know well that you adore me.

There're people who probably hate me,
it doesn't matter... with you, it's enough for me,
to continue fighting as I have until now,
I assure you that I won't fail you,
I won't disappear... as my shadow did.

MOTHERS

Today, the second Sunday of May,
it's a very special day.
Today is the birthday of all mothers,
who since always have been a source of happiness.
They're the ones who bring us into this world,
who take care of us
and give themselves up completely to such a task.
They always go out of their way for their children,
who are the reason for them to live and feel alive.
As they grow up, the children always leave,
looking for new horizons,
new adventures and a life to start.
Kids with big dreams,
who seek to find their reality.
Humans always continue to learn,
to be children, to be mothers.
The voice of triumph is in everyone,
and the most beautiful talent is being a mother,
it's incomparable... irresistibly adorable,
a being that gives life,
who lives for it without expecting anything in return!
Mothers are always attentive of us,
while we think about leaving the nest behind,
while their little ones grow up, and away they fly.

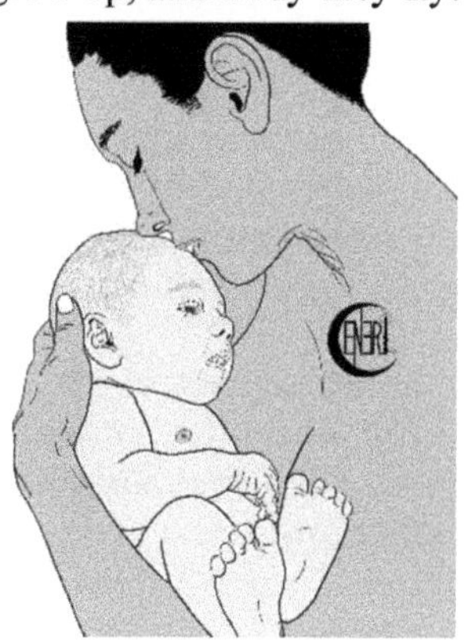

TRUE LOVE

We were two teenagers in a beautiful village
and we fell madly in love,
in that fair where I asked her for a date,
date that she didn't accept.

We went with friends to the movies,
without knowing that we would meet there.
We ended up walking back home under the night
and we broke the ice with laughter.

Every weekend we faced problems,
but our madness clung to us,
it was stronger than all tests.

The imposition of her parents
in the face of our love,
but they prefered the benefit and security of money.

It was our love of that summer...
in hopes that it become a forever,
after seven long years, you come back!
Looking for a response,
— Why didn't you look for me? She asked.
I wrote to you 365 times and from you,
I didn't hear back.

You come to me after so long,
and I know we can continue where we left,
let's live happily ever after,
let the world continue turning.

Love like ours no longer exists,
— you rebuilt this house for me,
here we will have children and grandchildren,
fruits of our love...

To end up in a hospital lost out of her mind,
that wasn't my plan, one more test for us,
something that depresses me but I won't give up losing her.

It was that script
of a lover clinging to his love,
to his beloved lover, who he loved all his life.

It was those readings...
memories that his beloved forgot,
it hurts to see that he doesn't remember you,
even more, when you carry him in your heart.

It's proven that nothing is forever,
but there was a love that lasted until death.

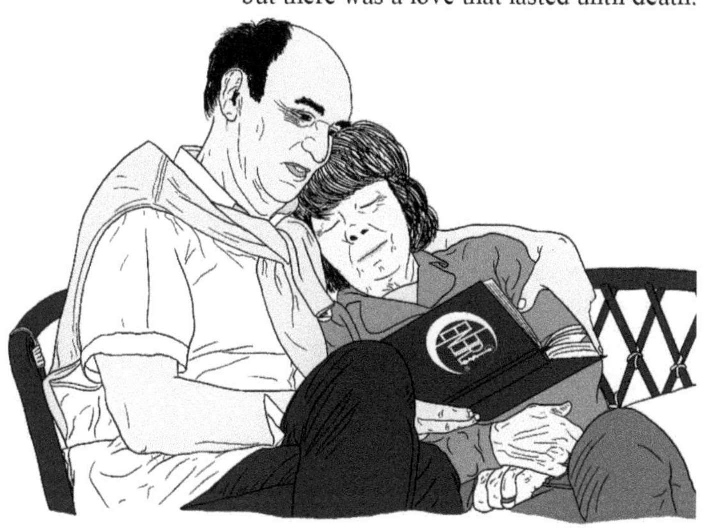

REFUSAL

I'm never going to break your heart,
don't doubt it,
it's just a matter of time.

I'm never going to make you cry.
How could I do such thing
if love you, oh beautiful wife?

I'm never going to let you fall,
no… it's not me who might try it,
how dare you accuse me after all.

I'll never tell you goodbye,
no, I can't… this isn't right.

I love you, even after I die,
you own my soul, my love and my life.

I'm not going to leave you,
not until God destroys my mind.

I refuse to leave you,
to live without your love in my life.

FEELINGS OF THE SOUL

Such beautiful expressions
sprout out the bottom of my soul!
These are beautiful sensations
that you inspire me with the way you look at me!
The desire to have you,
day, night, and dawn.
It's an inevitable sensation,
something indescribable...
You're like the shining star
that never goes out.
You're my path,
where I will rest in my shelter.
You're a love that means hope,
for me, my life, and my soul.
I just wanted you to know,
that my love is sincere and true.
And I wanted to tell you through these lines
to let you know what my soul feels,
emotions you inspire as I write this poetry,
which I dedicate to you expecting nothing in return.

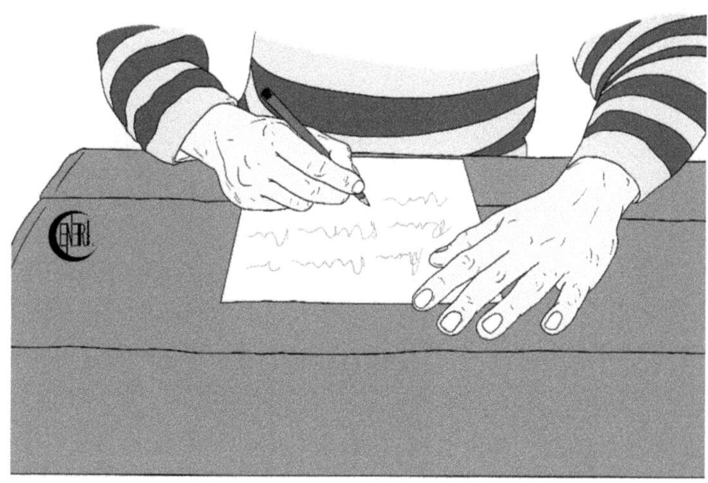

I DON'T ASK FOR MORE

At the beginning of my journey,
I ask no more than to have you in my soul.
Your rays of joy illuminate my path,
disappearing the gray sky of oblivion.

You're the reason of my joy every morning,
someone with whom I want to share my home.
Sin is inevitable in this century,
they all practice it; you all have a motive.

Let me be the reason why you sin,
let me show you what my heart feels.
You're a dream come true,
a story and a love poem.

A bright star in the immensity,
someone with whom I would like to have a better world.
You are a drop of water in a sea,
water that soothes my soul.

You're someone who seeks freedom,
someone with whom I can always be myself.

CHAPTER 9

VERSES
OF
LOVE

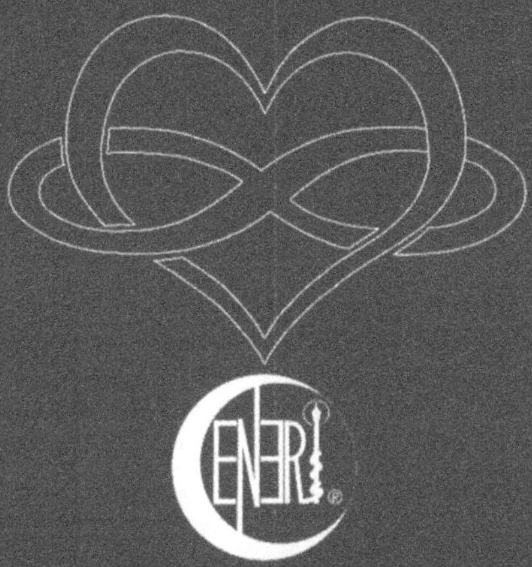

You know well that I love you
and in knowing it, you take advantage of my love,
because you know more than anyone that I love you
much more than my own life, my love...

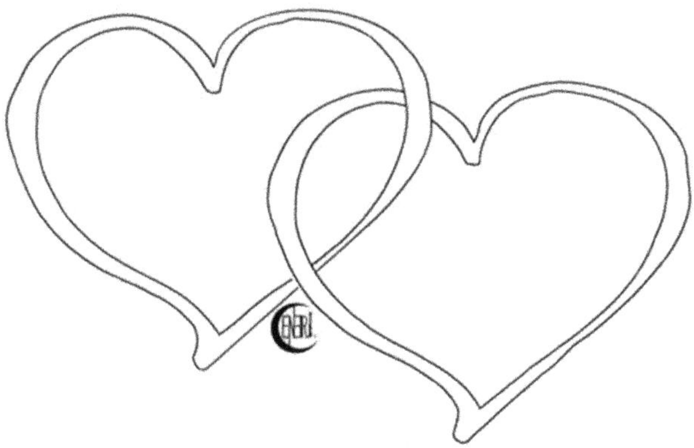

I have a hope inside my heart,
to see you one more time,
and even if you don't love me anymore,
I love you incessantly.

Your gaze is so beautiful
when you look at the palm trees,
I get lost in your light blue eyes,
like the clear water of the sea.

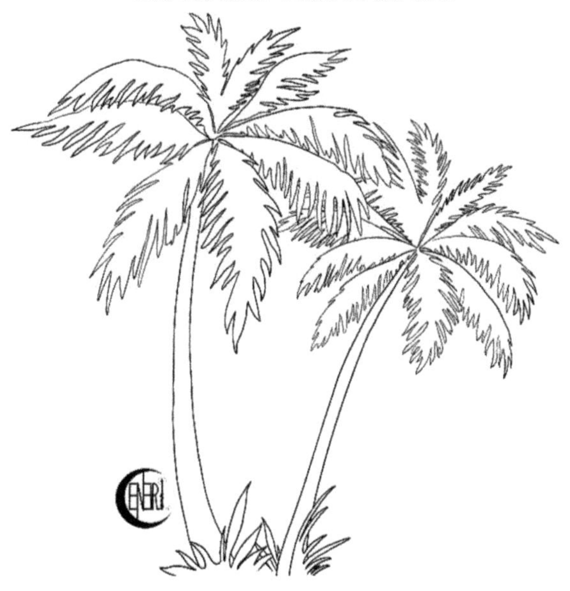

If the past didn't come back, I wouldn't worry…
and the things you knew would no longer scare me,
and maybe if I could,
without thinking I would even love you...

I can feel your presence,
when I fall asleep suffering,
and as I awake every morning,
I find new motives to live.

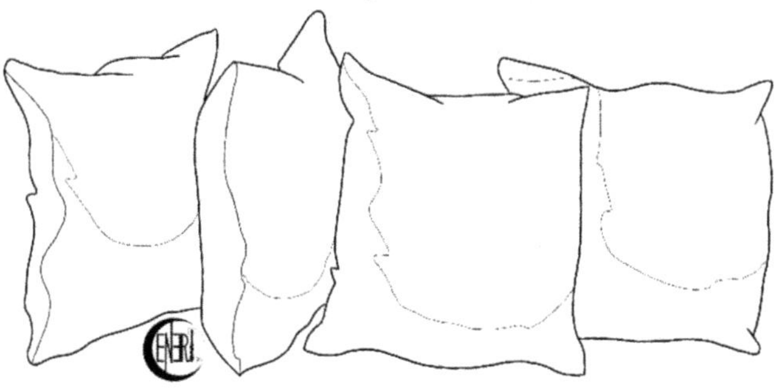

I'm moved by the way you look at me
because you glance at me and then go,
the way you look at me moves me
like a baby who stares at the rain.

The secrets and illusions,
are thoughts and feelings,
of events and passions,
that we keep in our hearts.

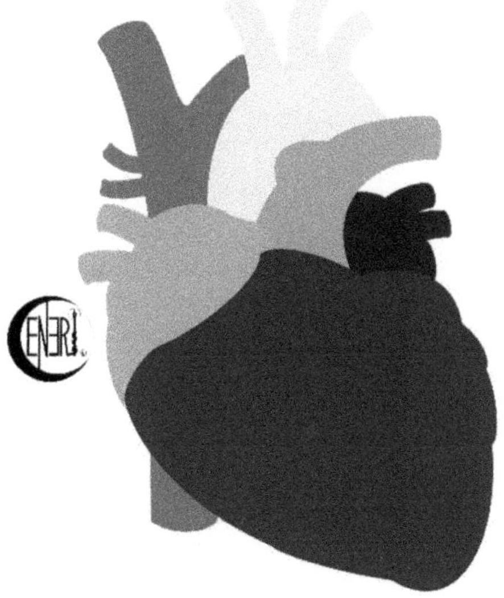

I think it's about time
to go outside and enjoy,
all possible moments;
of happiness, peace, and love.

My thoughts are up in the clouds
because I'm in love,
in love with a beautiful person,
that in my life I have found.

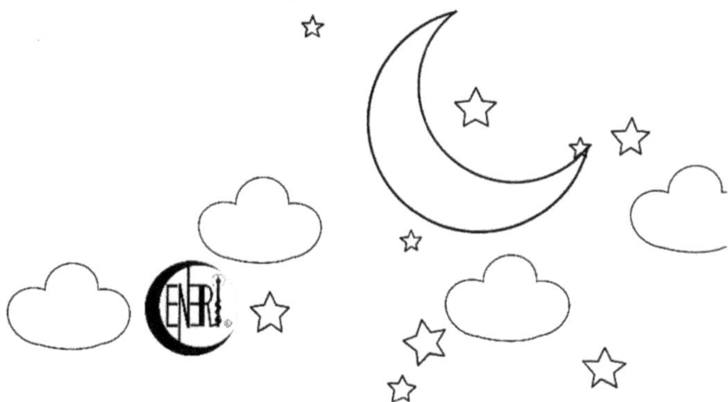

The words you say to me
they are really beautiful,
and although I know they are lies,
I love you with all my heart.

The reason of my existence
even I don't know it,
but loving for the first time,
it at least consoles me.

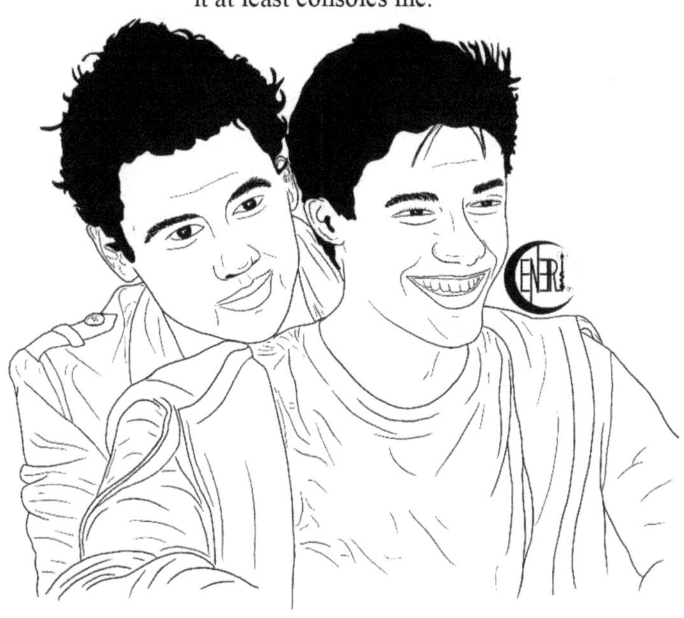

My anger motivates me
to live and to forget,
the little things of life
to not simply do them without cause.

These beautiful thoughts
to think that you would love me
without rejecting my kisses anymore
and love me more and more.

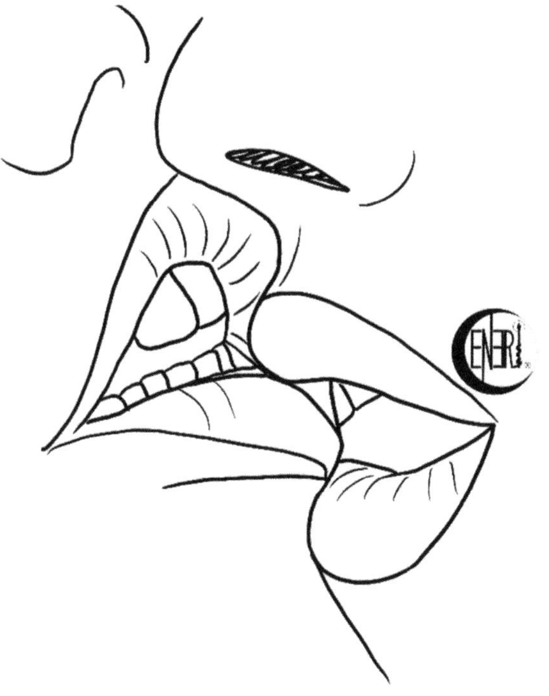

The person that I love
he's beautiful and much more,
and although people say otherwise
I don't care if it's true.

If you only dared to tell me how you feel,
if only I knew that you loved me since your met me,
maybe I wouldn't be where I am laying
and perhaps I would love you from now until forever.

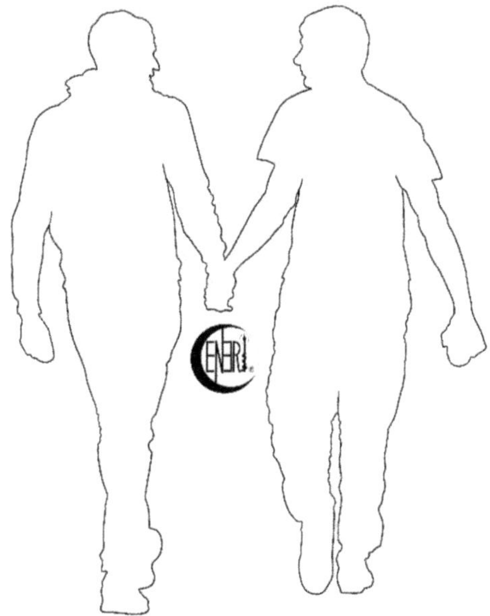

When I dream; I see you.
When I walk; I think of you.
When you kiss me; I love you.
and when you leave me, I miss you.

Your eyes are so beautiful
like two pearls of the sea,
shiny and vivid
like lighthouses in the sea.

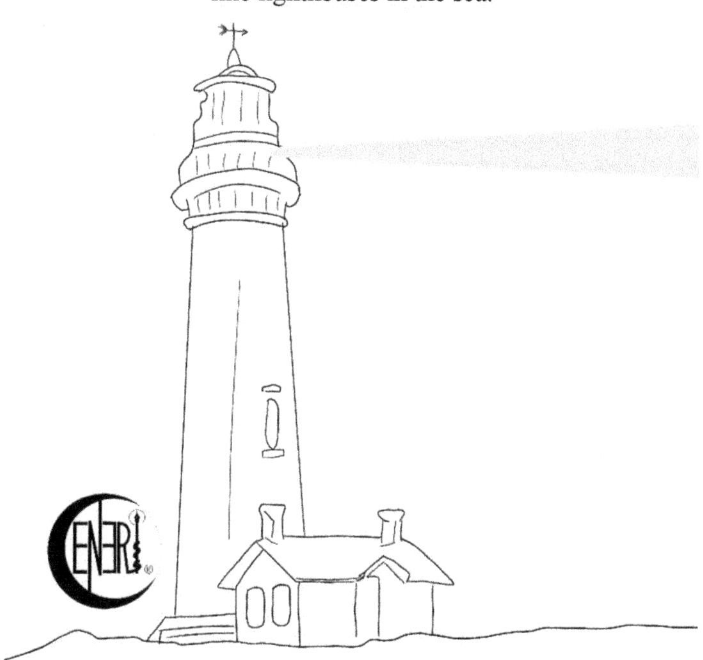

Having a perfect body doesn't matter,
what matters is what the heart feels,
because the body does not understand
how much is an illusion worth!

Women are gorgeous,
always as beautiful as roses,
romantic and tender,
and loving friends.

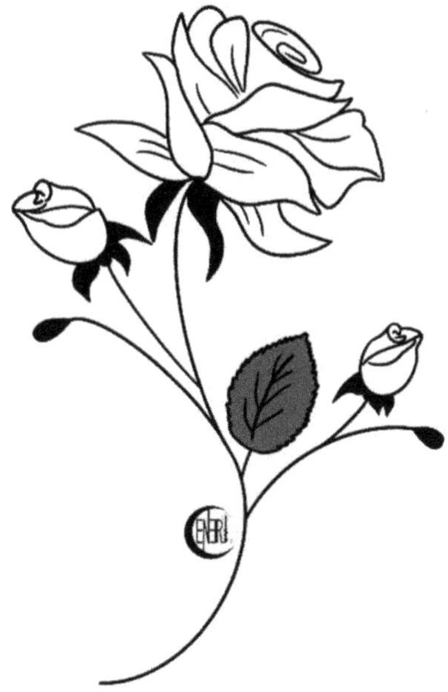

Adric Ceneri

The tears you shed
from your eyes with sensibility,
are because you love me
and you cry of sadness.

People don't understand,
that the body does not feel love...
and they also never fall for
those whom have a warm soul.

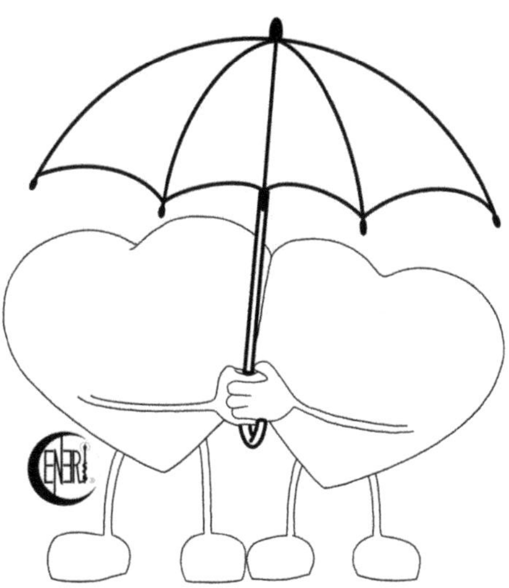

The mirror reflection
is the truth and the reason,
of the hidden secrets
that are guarded by our hearts.

The comets and stars
are torches of the moon,
that light the trails
of my life and yours.

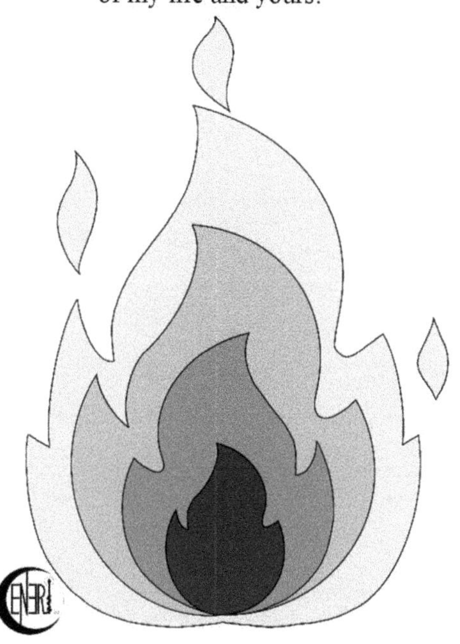

If you think I'm made of steel
you are very wrong,
I just play to be indifferent
like the infatuated devil.

Today I am close to you walking very happy,
but I'm not really here and you don't like me
that's why we better leave it like that,
so, I can keep dreaming that I am very happy.

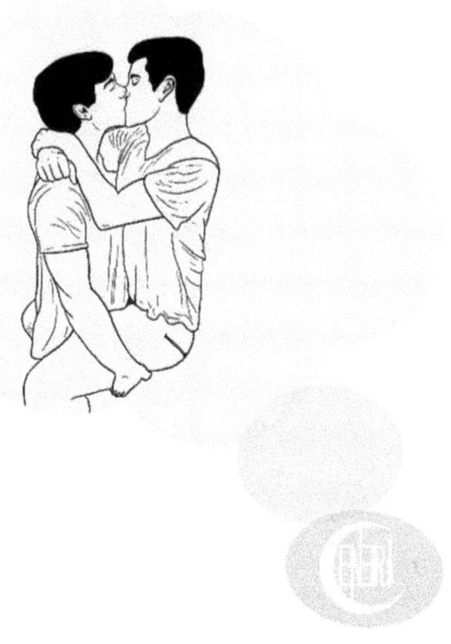

Shyness is in your eyes
I can see it all over your face,
and you get very nervous
when I look into your gaze.

You don't know how much I would give
for having you next to me,
and to tell you what I would do
to make you very happy.

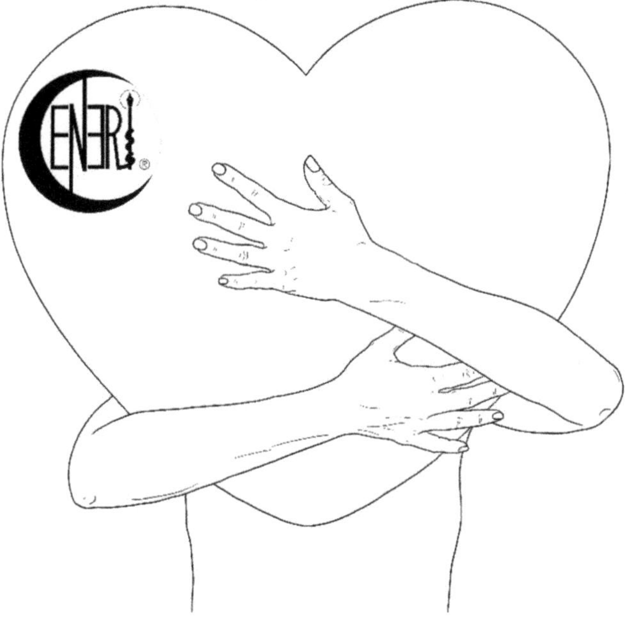

What a beautiful day,
seeing the glow,
of the rain that appears
around us.

There're times when hiding your feelings,
it's the best choice,
to avoid making a mistake that you will regret later,
and after hitting rock-bottom there will be no resignation
for the person who is suffering because of me.

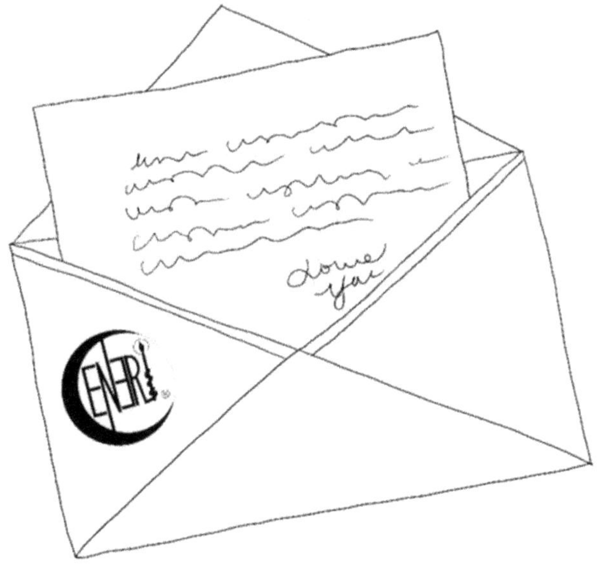

The rain is so beautiful
that reminds me of so many things,
some sad and some wonderful...
of my life that can be tragic and yet a gift.

The teddy bear that I gave to my mom,
on Mother's Day for being a very special day,
I always know that she loves me and without thinking,
I would give up my life to see her once more...

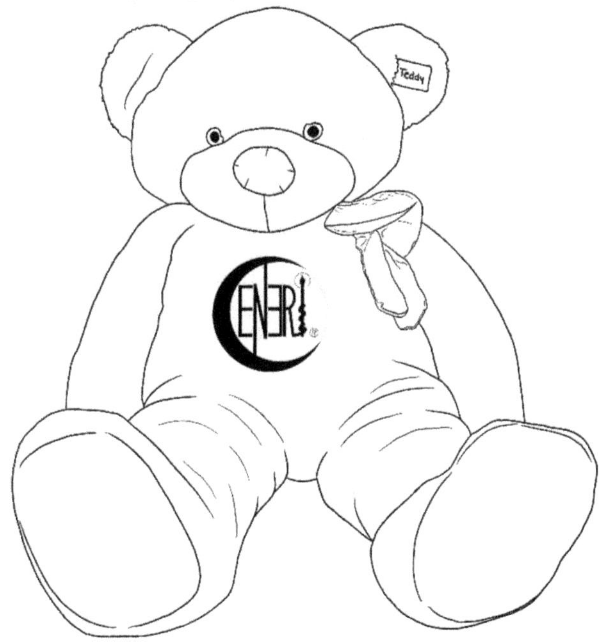

Despite the distance…
plains, mountains, deserts and beaches,
I will love you in this life
regardless of days and nights.

Here is my friendship; take it if you want it,
today in our first day, today in the nice of it.
Here is my way to live; I bet you, you can have it,
today in the best way, today in the safe of it.

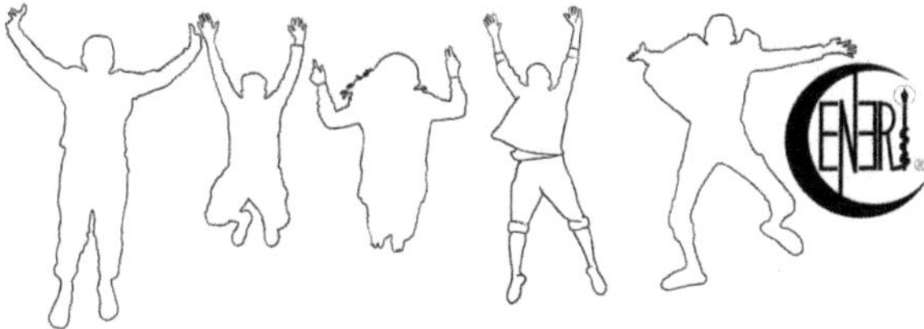

Wherever you are beware of everything,
and if you ever need my help, don't worry and reach out,
becuase I will be there to lend a hand,
and to care for you, whatever you need from me,
and so, we can remember the day when we met...

Today I want to dream
that you can love me,
that we can live together…
today, tomorrow and forever…

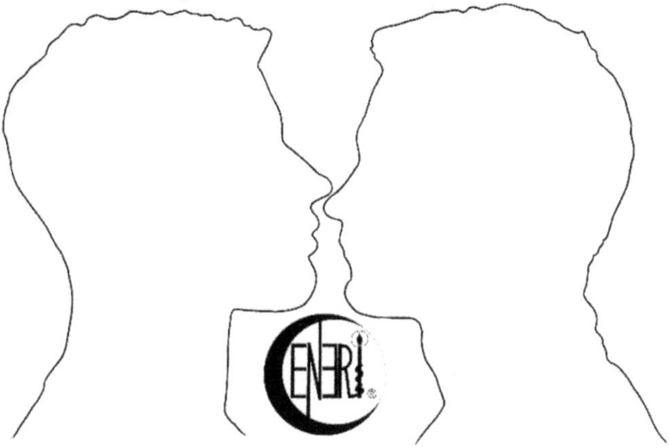

The dogs lived as a devil's god.
Disguised themselves as sweet pets,
yet animal instincts were dominant.
Sweet little creatures, not what we expect.

My illusion is gone
like my dreams when I wake up,
I want to sleep one more time
to dream with you in the stars.

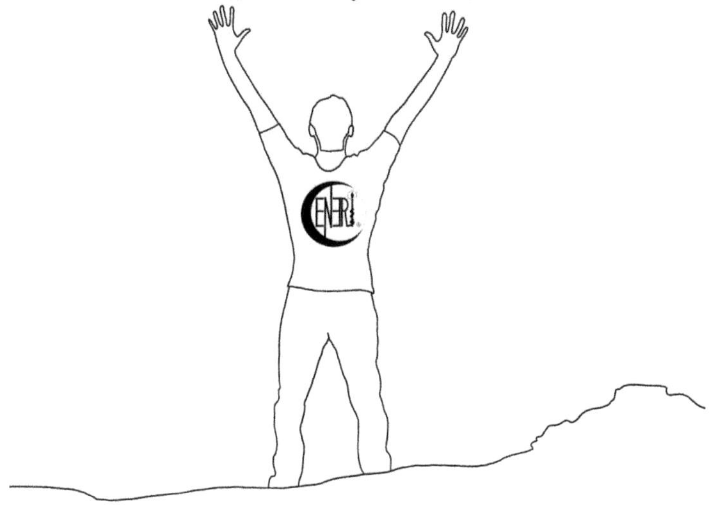

Adric Ceneri

My time is gone like the end of a song,
now I have to go, leaving you alone.
I hope you never forget our love,
and forever keep it into your mind and soul.

ABOUT THE AUTHOR

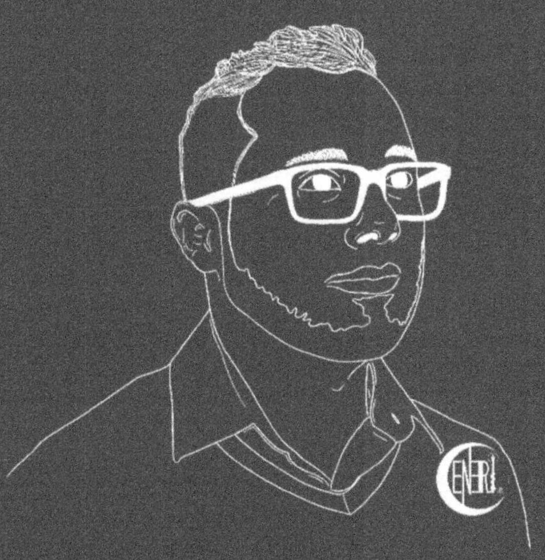

Adric Ceneri is an LGBTQ artist, poet, writer, and author. He was born in Mexico and lived there during his childhood. He was raised in the coasts of the Pacific Ocean with his parents up to the age of five, and when his parents separated, he had to endure and survive the consequences of his parents' poor life choices. The majority of his poetry reflects the pains and sufferings he had to endure. He writes about his sexuality and the events that marked him throughout childhood and the difficulties he faced when he was growing up. Ceneri often writes with a rebellious heart through his poetry, expressing his emotions and always remaining true to who he is as an artist. As a poet and writer, he transmits his feelings and embodies his transgressions in magical wordplays truly transforming pain into art.

In August of 2003, Ceneri moved to the U.S. with his family seeking shelter for peace from the torment that had poisoned him and pushed him to attempt taking his own life. After surviving the horrors of what he had to live, his mind and soul were deeply corrupted and he got broken beyond repair.

As a coping mechanism, he began writing after school during his high school years. While he was concentrated in learning a new language in a foreign land, he was also motivated to explore his creativity and discover a new side of him in his art class. He became passionate for art; and art in general became the coping mechanism that helped him survive through his teenage years.

With over 17 years writing and over 10 years since his birth as a published poet and writer; Ceneri ha now 2 poetry collections and a set of four-book journals.

Ceneri is currently invested in Magesoul Publishing working with the founder, Carlos Medina and core executives to help the poetry community voices to be heard and recognized.

Adric is a passionate artist, creating books covers such as 'IT HURTS', 'SURVIVAL' and 'HEALING', the first trilogy of anthologies by Magesoul Publishing and other books published through Magesoul Publishing. Adric also has written a chapter for each of these books, poems that aren't published in any of his other books. He is also translating books and creating art for other authors.

Check his website:
www.adricceneri.com

And don't forget to connect with him in social media:

Instagram @adricceneriwrites @booksbyceneri
Twitter @adricceneri
Facebook Page @adricceneriwrites
Tumblr @ adricceneriwrites
YouTube Channel: **Adric Ceneri**

OTHER BOOKS

by Adric Ceneri

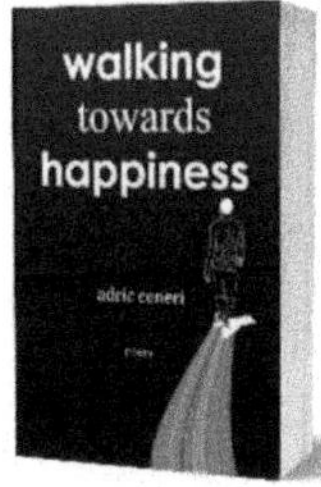

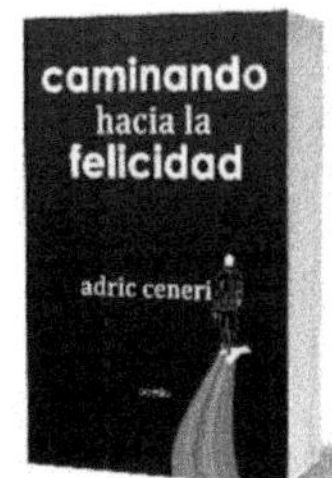

Walking Towards Happiness *(English and Spanish)*

This book is a collection of poetry along with graphic art to provide a vivid picture of these meaningful words. An amazing book of storytelling poetry, which shares the story of the author's life experience throughout time in seven phases.

I am simply content with my life's journey and this book tells the story of these last years; living in the darkness that I carry in me, expressing my lust and the desires I lived lost in the damnation of the ignorant but I rise up and found in my utter poetry a reason to chase my happiness above all and I woke up one day to find my heart beating in love again.

— Adric Ceneri

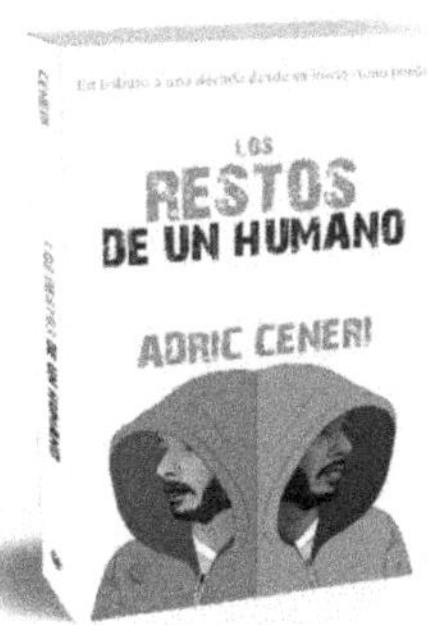

Los Restos de un Humano *(Spanish version)*

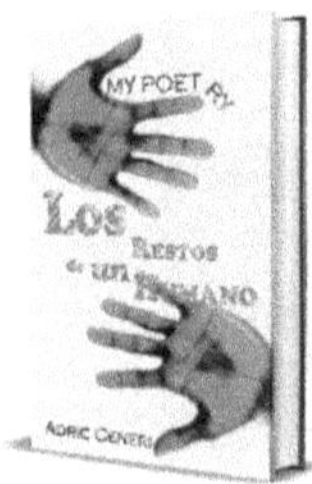 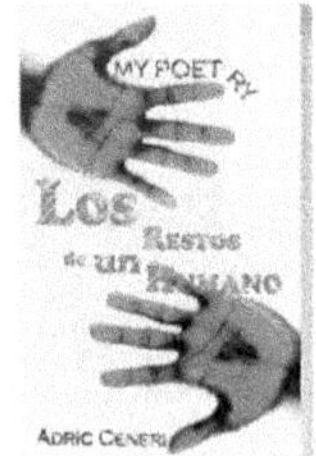

MY POETRY:
Los Restos de un Humano
(Bilingual version)

A poetry collection filled with secrets and experiences.
Pieces of memories and images which create these verses with
my illusions among the lines and confusing riddles between my
rhymes. Magical paths that are a true divine gift, but sometimes
it can also be a dangerous labyrinth for those who do not
understand the difference between the real world and my
fantasies.

Books by Magesoul Publishing

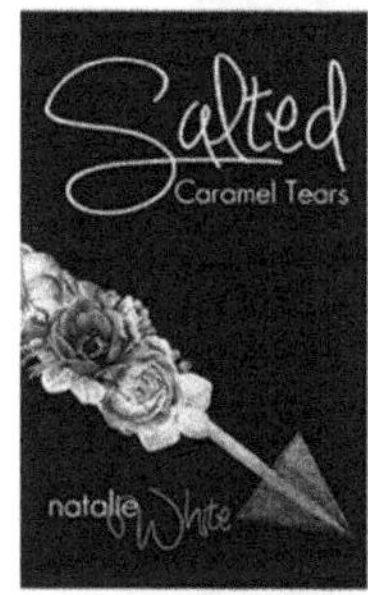
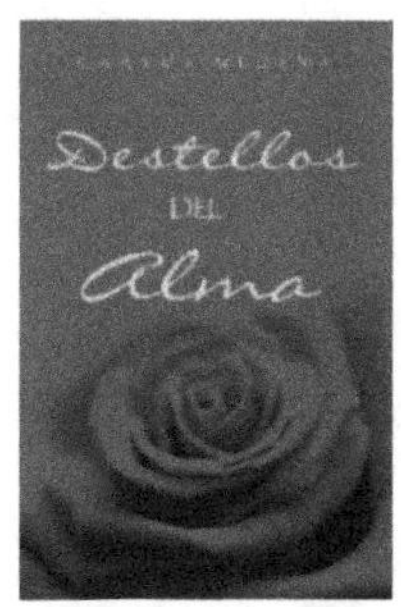
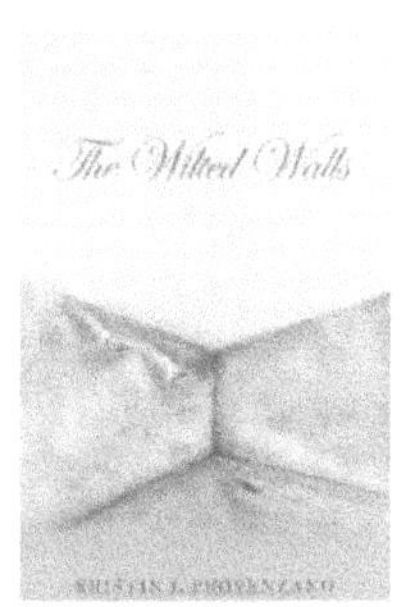

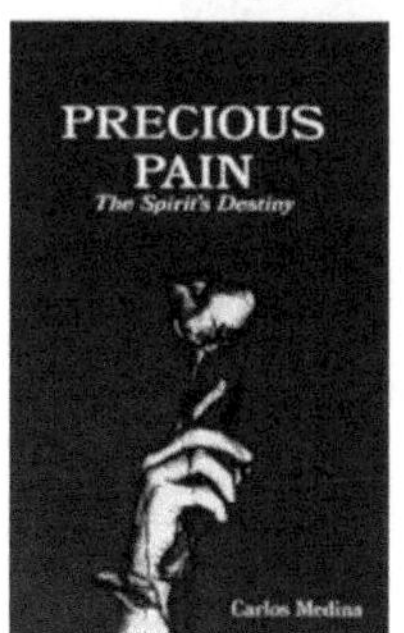
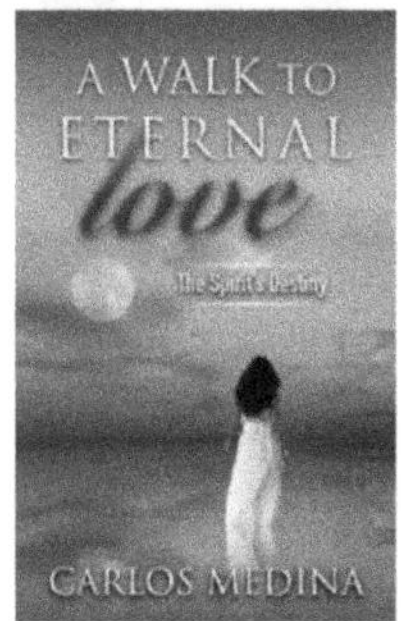
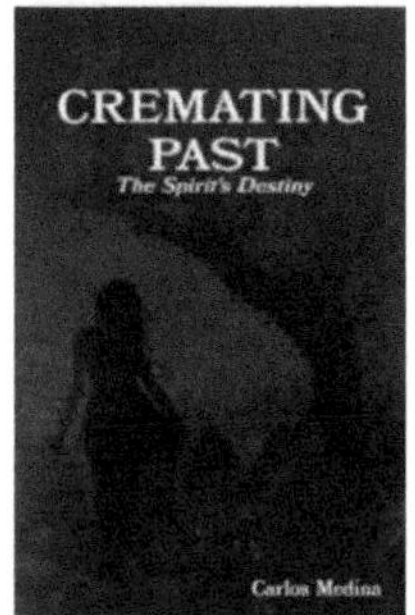

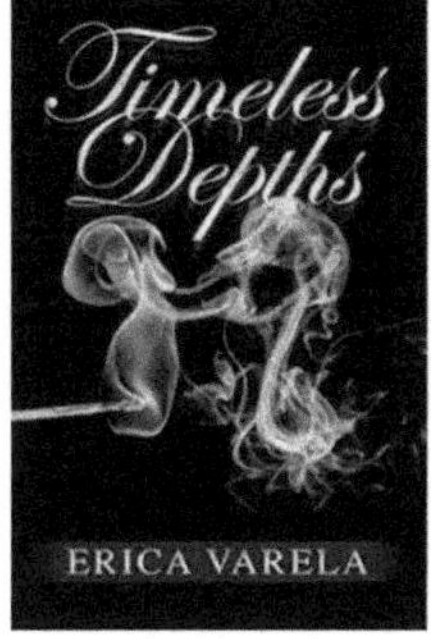

Coming Soon to Magesoul Publishing

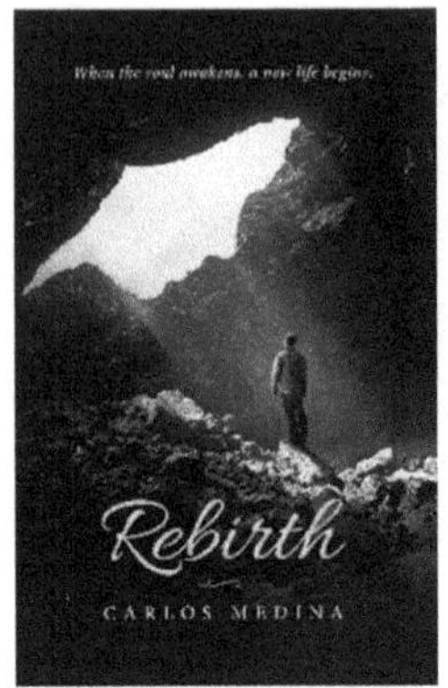

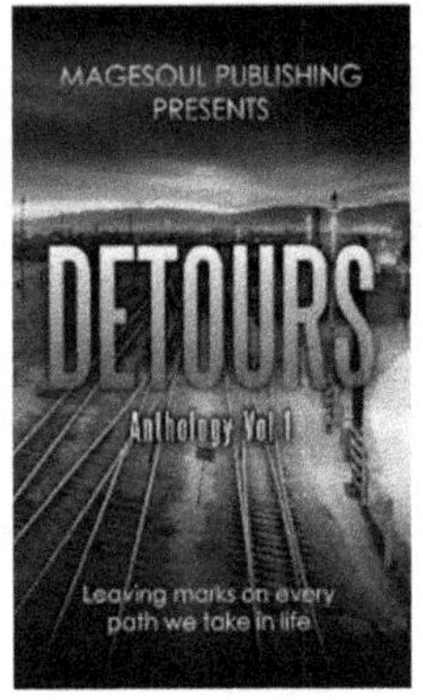

9 781734 290868